About the Author

Mr. Paul Watson has many years of experience in working with Selenium Webdriver, Junit, TestNG and Cucumber. He has worked on large software projects in USA, UK, Singapore, Hong Kong, Dubai, Australia and Switzerland.

His hobbies include travelling to new tourist places, watching basketball, cricket, Soccer and learning latest technological stuff.

Who is this book for

This book is for software developers, automation testers, Devops and engineers working on selenium automation testing project. Whether you are a beginner or an experienced developer, this book will help you master the skills on Selenium.

The book starts with introduction of Selenium and then dives into key concepts like setting up project in IntelliJ, integration with Junit and TestNG, integration with build tools like Gradle and Maven. You will also learn how to integrate selenium with Cucumber. In the end, you will learn how to run the Selenium tests on CI servers like TeamCity, Bamboo and Jenkins. You will also learn how to work with various types of frameworks like Page object models, Page factory Keyword driven frameworks etc. Book also touches the concepts related to mobile automation using Selenium.

Preface

In this book, you will find all concepts related to Selenium Webdriver.

You will learn below topics.

1. Introduction
2. Selenium Architecture
3. Webdriver JSON Wire protocol
4. Installation, Browsers
5. Capabilities
6. Basic operations
7. Element identification methods
8. Element operations
9. Synchronization
10. Advanced XPATH and CSS expressions
11. Working with tables
12. Handling multiple browser windows
13. Exceptions
14. Switching contexts
15. JavascriptExecutor
16. Frameworks with selenium – Junit and TestNG
17. BDD frameworks - Cucumber
18. Integration with CI servers like Bamboo, TeamCity and Jenkins
19. Selenium in Cloud
20. Mobile application testing
21. Selenium grid
22. Comparing selenium with other tools
23. Challenges in Selenium automation

1. Introduction

Selenium web driver is the most popular browser automation testing tool. Project is hosted at https://github.com/seleniumhq/selenium.

Key features of Selenium Webdriver are -

Open source

1. Supports all major browsers - IE, Firefox, Chrome, Safari, Opera
2. API is available in all popular languages like Java, Groovy, C#, PHP, Python etc.
3. Selenium Webdriver is a W3C standard protocol for Browser Automation
4. Supports testing for Desktop web applications, iOS and Android mobile applications
5. Testing web applications on emulated mobile devices is possible using mobile emulation in chrome

For every web browser, there is a separate web driver implementation that helps us automate the browser operations.

For example ->

If you want to automate chrome, you will need chromedriver. Chromedriver is an application file that is used to perform the operations on browser.Similarly for firefox and Internet Explorer there are different drivers.

```
System.setProperty("webdriver.chrome.driver",
"C:\\chromedriver.exe");
WebDriver driver =  new ChromeDriver();
```

Above code will create new web driver reference that can be used to automate the test cases on chrome browser.

```
File profileDir = new
File("C:\\Users\\Firefox\\Profiles\\default");
 FirefoxProfile profile = new
FirefoxProfile(profileDir);
 wb =  new FirefoxDriver(profile);
```

Above code will launch firefox.

2. Selenium Architecture

You will get to know the Selenium Webdriver architectural diagram.

Before you take a look at diagram, kindly note below points.

1. Selenium webdriver uses JSON WIRE protocol over well known HTTP protocol.
2. Your automation code sends HTTP commands to Webdriver Server (IEDriverServer.exe or ChromeDriver.exe).
3. Webdriver Server (IEDriverServer.exe or ChromeDriver.exe) sends these commands to the browser under test through HTTP proxy.
4. Browser under test executes the commands sent by Webdriver Server and sends the results back to the Webdriver Server.
5. Webdriver server interprets the results and your automation code takes further action on those results.

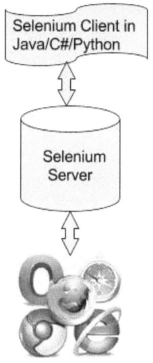

3. Webdriver JSON Wire protocol

Did you ever wonder how Selenium 2.0 works internally? In this post, you will get to know how selenium automates the browser.

Selenium API sends HTTP commands in the form of JSON protocol to Selenium Server.
Selenium server then uses native browser API to automate the browser.

So when use below statement in your code –

```
driver = new ChromeDriver();
```

It actually sends the below HTTP command to the selenium server.

POST /session

For each selenium API method, there is a corresponding HTTP request that is sent to the server. Here is the list of some of the HTTP commands that are sent to Selenium Server.

1. POST /session - Create new session
2. GET /status - Get the state of server
3. DELETE /session/:sessionId - Delete the session with id - sessionId

4. POST /session/:sessionId/timeouts/implicit_wait - Specify the amount of time the driver should wait when searching for elements.

5. GET /session/:sessionId/url - Navigate to the specific url

Below image demonstrates how the JSON protocol works in Selenium.

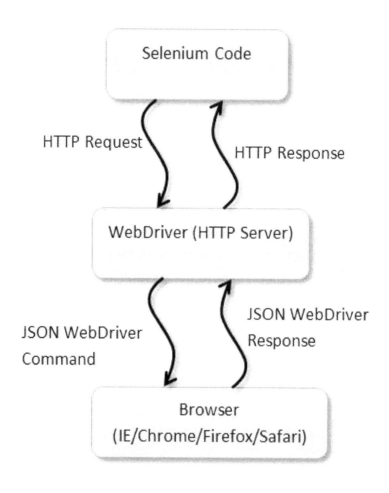

4. Installation

4.1 Install the web driver for chrome, firefox

To start automating the test cases with selenium, you need to follow below steps.

Assuming that you will choose Java as a programming language for selenium automation, you will need below things.

Below is the list of softwares you will need ->

1. Selenium API (Jar file) - http://docs.seleniumhq.org/download/
2. Webdriver for Interenet Explorer
3. Webdriver for Chrome
4. Eclipse - Java IDE

Once you have these softwares with you, You can follow below steps.

1. Open Eclipse and create new Java Project.
2. Create a package and class with name SampleTest in it.
3. Go to project properties and select Java build path. Select libraries tab and then choose add external jar.
4. Browse to the jar file you have downloaded in step 1 first list.
5. Select apply and close

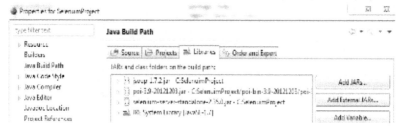

Add Selenium API library to Eclipse IDE

4.2 Setting up Selenium and Maven project

In Maven project, you can add below dependency and start writing the tests in JUnit or TestNG framework.

```
<dependency>

<groupId>org.seleniumhq.selenium</groupId>
        <artifactId>selenium-java</artifactId>
        <version>2.53.1</version>
</dependency>
```

4.3 Setting up Selenium Gradle project in Intellij IDEA

Gradle is one of the most popular build management systems in the Java world. Gradle is developed to eliminate the drawbacks in Ant and Maven. In this article, you will learn how you can set up a selenium project using Gradle in Intellij IDEA.

The tools you will need are -

1. JDK - You can know more about JDK installation process in Windows on Softpost Java Tutorial
2. Intellij IDEA IDE - Community Edition (It's free)
3. Gradle (It's free) In latest versions of Intellij IDEA (15.0.4+) , Gradle comes built-in So you do not need to download it separately.

Below Images will guide you through the steps for creating the Selenium-Gradle project.

Step 1 - Click on New Project menu in Intellij IDEA and then select Gradle Project

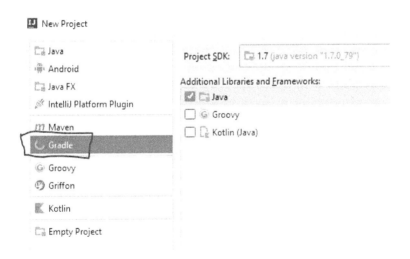

Step 2 - Types in the Group Id and Artifact Id for your project

New Project

GroupId	org.softpost
ArtifactId	gradleselenium|
Version	1.0-SNAPSHOT

Step 3 - Provide Gradle Settings

New Project

- ☑ Use auto-import
- ☑ Create directories for empty content roots automatically
- ⦿ Use default gradle wrapper (recommended)
- ○ Use customizable gradle wrapper ⓘ Gradle wrapper customization in script, works with Grad
- ○ Use local gradle distribution

Gradle home:

Gradle JVM: ⬚ 1.7 (java version "1.7.0_79", path: C:/Pro

Step 4 - Type Project Name

New Project

Project name: gradleselenium|

Project location: C:\Users\Sagar\IdeaProjects\gradleselenium

Step 5 - Gradle project directory layout

Step 6 - Build.Gradle File and Selenium dependency

```
gradleselenium ×    TestClass.java ×

group 'org.softpost'
version '1.0-SNAPSHOT'

apply plugin: 'java'

sourceCompatibility = 1.5

repositories {
    mavenCentral()
}

dependencies {
    testCompile group: 'junit', name: 'junit', version: '4.11'
    testCompile group: 'org.seleniumhq.selenium', name: 'selenium-java', version: '2.53.0'
}
```

Step 7 - Write and execute Selenium tests

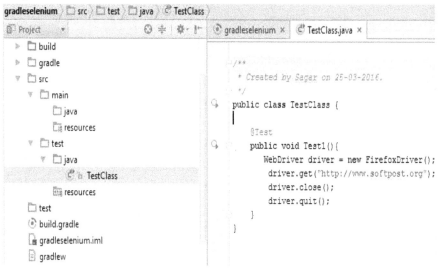

Step 8 - Executing gradle tasks

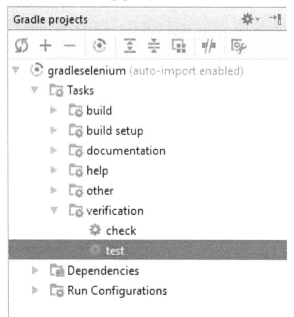

5. Browsers

5.1 Launch internet explorer browser

You can download the IE driver from the link -
http://docs.seleniumhq.org/download/. IEDriverServer
supports 32 bit as well as 64 bit Internet Explorer.

Setting the driver parameters

Ensure that Server path is included in System PATH
variable or set the property as shown below.

```
System.setProperty("webdriver.ie.driver",
"F:\\selenium\\java\\iedriver.exe");
```

Other properties that we can set are given below.

1. webdriver.ie.driver.host
2. webdriver.ie.driver.loglevel
3. webdriver.ie.driver.logfile
4. webdriver.ie.driver.silent

Browser Settings

Ensure that Protected mode settings for all zones should
be same and for IE10 and above, enhanced protected
mode must be disabled and the browser zoom level must
be set to 100%.

For IE 11 only, You will need to edit below registry keys.

For 32-bit Windows, the key is HKEY_LOCAL_MACHINE\SOFTWARE\Microsoft\Internet Explorer\Main\FeatureControl\FEATURE_BFCACHE. For 64-bit Windows, the key is HKEY_LOCAL_MACHINE\SOFTWARE\Wow6432Node\Micr osoft\Internet Explorer\Main\FeatureControl\FEATURE_BFCACHE.

Please note that the FEATURE_BFCACHE subkey is optional and and should be created if not present. Inside this key, you need to create a DWORD value with name = iexplore.exe and value = 0.

To clean IE Session

Ensure that you pass below capability - ie.ensureCleanSession with true value.

Example code to launch IE

You can use below example/code to start the new IE session in Java using selenium web driver.

```
package seleniumtest;

import java.util.concurrent.TimeUnit;

import org.openqa.selenium.By;
import org.openqa.selenium.Keys;
import org.openqa.selenium.WebDriver;
import org.openqa.selenium.WebElement;
import org.openqa.selenium.chrome.ChromeDriver;
import org.openqa.selenium.ie.*;
import org.openqa.selenium.interactions.Action;
import org.openqa.selenium.interactions.Actions
;

public  class MainTest
{


     public static void main(String[] args)
      {

         WebDriver driver =null;
         System.setProperty("webdriver.ie.dri
ver", "F:\\selenium\\java\\iedriver.exe");
         driver = new InternetExplorerDriver();
         driver.manage().timeouts().pageLoadTim
eout(20, TimeUnit.SECONDS);
         driver.manage().timeouts().implicitlyW
ait(20, TimeUnit.SECONDS);


         try
         {

      driver.get("http://register.rediff.com/
register/register.php");
      driver.findElement(By.name("name")).sen
dKeys("ff89");
```

```
        driver.findElement(By.name("name")).sen
dKeys(Keys.TAB);
        Thread.sleep(3000);

        //driver.findElement(By.name("passwd"))
.click();
        Actions builder = new Actions(driver);


        WebElement e =
driver.findElement(By.cssSelector("#sk"));
        //build the action chain.
                        Action doubleclick =
builder.doubleClick(e).build();

        //perform the double click action
        doubleclick.perform();


        driver.switchTo().alert().accept();
        Thread.sleep(4000);
        //driver.navigate();
   //driver.navigate("http://www.google.com");

        }
     catch(Exception e)
     {

     System.out.println(e.toString());
     }

     finally
      {
        driver.close();
        driver.quit();
      }
     }
}
```

Please note that we need to set the system property webdriver.ie.driver

We have to give the path of IEdriver.exe

Once you have created driver object, you can use its methods to automated the browser tasks.

5.2 Launch chrome browser

Desired Capabilities of ChromeDriver

Chrome can be configured in various ways as mentioned by Google developer.

```
ChromeOptions options = new ChromeOptions();

//using chrome binary from specific location
options.setBinary("/path/to/other/chrome/binary
");

//Setting the chrome profile
options.addArguments("user-data-
dir=/path/to/your/profile");

//to disable pop up blocking
options.addArguments("disable-popup-blocking");

//To start chrome without security warning
options.addArguments("test-type");

//To start the chrome in Maximized mode
options.addArguments("start-maximized");

//Setting custom options
Map<String, Object> prefs = new HashMap<String,
Object>();
```

```
prefs.put("profile.default_content_settings.pop
ups", 0);
options.setExperimentalOption("prefs", prefs);

//Adding extensions to chrome
options.addExtensions(new
File("/path/to/extension.crx"));

We can directly pass the options to driver as
shown below

driver = new ChromeDriver(options);

Or we can also set the capabilities as shown
below

DesiredCapabilities capabilities = new
DesiredCapabilities();
capabilities.setCapability(ChromeOptions.CAPABI
LITY, options);
ChromeDriver driver = new
ChromeDriver(capabilities);
```

Mobile emulation using ChromeDriver

You can start the chrome in mobile emulation mode by passing below capabilities.Please note that you can pass any device name as shown in chrome developer tools.

```
Map<String, String> mobileEmulation = new
HashMap<String, String>();
mobileEmulation.put("deviceName", "Google Nexus
7");

Map<String, Object> chromeOptions = new
HashMap<String, Object>();
chromeOptions.put("mobileEmulation",
mobileEmulation);
```

Using RemoteWebDriver and ChromeDriver

You can start the chromedriver as shown below.

$ ./chromedriver

Started ChromeDriver

port=9515

Then you can use below code to instantiate the driver.

```
WebDriver driver = new
RemoteWebDriver("http://127.0.0.1:9515",
DesiredCapabilities.chrome());
driver.get("http://www.softpost.org");
```

ChromeDriver Example

You can use below example/code to start the new chrome session in Java using selenium web driver.

```
package seleniumtest;

import java.util.concurrent.TimeUnit;

import org.openqa.selenium.By;
import org.openqa.selenium.Keys;
import org.openqa.selenium.WebDriver;
import org.openqa.selenium.WebElement;
import org.openqa.selenium.chrome.ChromeDriver;
import org.openqa.selenium.ie.*;
import org.openqa.selenium.interactions.Action;
import org.openqa.selenium.interactions.Actions
;
```

```java
public  class MainTest
{

    public static void main(String[] args)
    {

      WebDriver driver =null;
      System.setProperty("webdriver.chrome.driv
er",  "F:\\selenium\\csharp\\chromedriver.exe");
      driver = new ChromeDriver();
      driver.manage().timeouts().pageLoadTimeou
t(20, TimeUnit.SECONDS);
      driver.manage().timeouts().implicitlyWait
(20, TimeUnit.SECONDS);

       try
       {
         driver.get("http://register.rediff.com
/register/register.php");
driver.findElement(By.name("name")).sendKeys("f
f89");

         Thread.sleep(4000);
         //driver.navigate();
    //driver.navigate("http://www.google.com");

       }
       catch(Exception e)
        {

          System.out.println(e.toString());
       }
       finally
        {
          driver.close();
          driver.quit();
        }
    }
}
```

Please note that we need to set the system property webdriver.chrome.driver

We have to give the path of chromedriver exe

Once you have created driver object, you can use its methods to automated the browser tasks.

5.3 Launching Firefox browser

To launch the Firefox using Selenium, you do not need to download and run the Firefox driver separately. Below line of code will start the Firefox from standard location.

```
WebDriver driver = new
FirefoxDriver(myprofile);
```

Using different Firefox profile

```
ProfilesIni profile = new ProfilesIni();

FirefoxProfile myprofile =
profile.getProfile("XYZ");
caps.setCapability(FirefoxDriver.PROFILE,
profile);
```

Or you can also create new profile on the fly and pass that capability as shown in below code.

```
FirefoxProfile profile = new FirefoxProfile();
profile.setPreference("plugin.state.flash", 1);
caps.setCapability(FirefoxDriver.PROFILE,
profile);
```

Using specific Firefox binary

Sometimes, we need to execute the tests on specific version of Firefox. We can download portable firefox from https://sourceforge.net/projects/portableapps/files/ Mozilla%20Firefox%2C%20Portable%20Ed./ and run that binary as shown in below code.

```
File pathToBinary = new
File("c:\\FirefoxPortable_p.exe");
FirefoxBinary ffBinary = new
FirefoxBinary(pathToBinary);
FirefoxProfile firefoxProfile = new
FirefoxProfile();
WebDriver driver = new
FirefoxDriver(ffBinary,firefoxProfile);
```

5.4 Launching Microsoft Edge Browser

We can launch the Microsoft Edge Browser using below code. Note that you will have to download the Microsoft Edge driver from the link -
 https://www.microsoft.com/en-us/download/details.aspx?id=48740 and set the property - webdriver.edge.driver in code. Also make sure that you are aware of IE settings required for Selenium.

```
package msedgetests;

import org.junit.Test;
import org.openqa.selenium.JavascriptExecutor;
import org.openqa.selenium.WebDriver;
import org.openqa.selenium.edge.EdgeDriver;
```

```java
import
org.openqa.selenium.ie.InternetExplorerDriver;

import java.util.concurrent.TimeUnit;

/**
 * Created by Sagar on 19-02-2016.
 */
public class LaunchEdge
{

    @Test
    public void launchEdgeBrowser() throws
Exception
    {
        WebDriver driver = null;

System.setProperty("webdriver.edge.driver",
        "C:\\Program Files (x86)\\Microsoft Web
Driver\\MicrosoftWebDriver.exe");

        driver = new EdgeDriver();

driver.manage().timeouts().implicitlyWait(10,
TimeUnit.SECONDS);
        driver.manage().window().maximize();
        String domain =
"http://www.softpost.org";
        driver.get(domain);
        System.out.println(driver.getTitle());
        driver.close();
        driver.quit();
    }
}
```

5.5 Launching Safari browser

Before automating the Safari Browser, ensure that you do below settings.

1. Create Safari Extension developer certificate on Apple developer website.
2. Install webdriver extension in Safari Browser. You can download webdriver extension http://selenium-release.storage.googleapis.com/index.html?path=2.48/

Below image shows the sample extension on the google site.

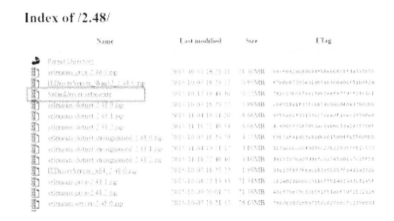

Below code will launch the Safari browser.

```
Webdriver driver = new SafariDriver();
driver.get("http://www.softpost.org");
```

5.6 Headless execution using HTML Unit

Headless mean without any user interface. HtmlUnit allows you to execute tests in Headless manner. You will not see browser opening the web pages or performing any operation like clicking buttons or entering data. All these operations happen in memory. This kind of execution is useful if you want to test the functionality. Also headless execution is much faster than normal execution. Downside is that you will not be able to test how the web page actually looks like on specific browser.

You will have to add below dependency in your project.

```
<dependency>
    <groupId>org.apache.httpcomponents</groupId>
    <artifactId>httpclient</artifactId>
    <version>4.5.2</version>
</dependency>
```

By default, JavaScript is not enabled. You need to use below line to execute JavaScript.

```
((HtmlUnitDriver)driver).setJavascriptEnabled(true);
```

Here is the complete code to execute selenium tests using HtmlUnitDriver.

```
package htmlunit;

import org.openqa.selenium.WebDriver;
import
org.openqa.selenium.htmlunit.HtmlUnitDriver;

/**
 * Created by Sagar on 21-06-2016.
 */
public class testHtmlUnit
{
    public static void main(String[] args)
    {
        WebDriver driver = new
HtmlUnitDriver();
        driver.get("http://www.softpost.org");
        driver.close();
        driver.quit();
    }
}
```

6. Capabilities

6.1 Selenium Webdriver Capabilities Significance

In Selenium, we have a Webdriver Interface and there are lot of classes that implement this interface.
So let us first try to understand this interface.

What is inside this WebDriver Interface?
Important methods declared inside this interface are -

1. get
2. findElement
3. getTitle
4. getPageSource....etc

The classes that implement this interface are given below.

1. ChromeDriver
2. EventFiringWebDriver
3. FirefoxDriver
4. HtmlUnitDriver
5. InternetExplorerDriver
6. OperaDriver
7. RemoteWebDriver
8. SafariDriver

Now let us take a look at different constructors for ChromeDriver.

1. ChromeDriver()
2. ChromeDriver(Capabilities capabilities)
3. ChromeDriver(ChromeDriverService service)
4. ChromeDriver(ChromeDriverService service, Capabilities capabilities)
5. ChromeDriver(ChromeDriverService service, ChromeOptions options)
6. ChromeDriver(ChromeOptions options)

As you can see, in Java Selenium API, we have 6 constructors for the ChromeDriver class.

The first constructor takes no arguments. But rest of them are taking the arguments as mentioned below.

1. Capabilities
2. ChromeDriverService
3. ChromeOptions

Now let us try to understand the significance of these classes.

Capabilities are used to manage the browser attributes. For example - we can set the browser name, version, platform using capabilities.

ChromeDriverService is used to manage the chrome server (exe). Finally, ChromeOptions are used to set the options specific to the chrome browser like adding extensions, setting the binary path etc.

Constructors for other classes also take similar arguments as mentioned above.

Capabilities used by Selenium Server

1. browserName - chrome|firefox|internet explorer|htmlunit|android|iPhone|iPad|opera|safari
2. version
3. platform - WINDOWS|MAC|LINUX|UNIX|ANDROID

Some other important Capabilities

1. acceptSslCerts
2. nativeEvents
3. proxy

IE specific Capabilities

1. ignoreZoomSetting
2. ie.ensureCleanSession

Firefox specific Capabilities

1. firefox_binary

7. Basic operations

7.1 Closing browser window

Below example shows how we can close the browser window in java using selenium web driver

```
WebDriver driver = new FirefoxDriver();
driver.close();
driver.quit();
```

Please note that same code will work on all other browsers like chrome, safari and IE. Notice that same code can be used to close the tabs as well. A tab in browser is considered as a new browser window in Selenium.

7.2 Navigating to url

Here is the sample program that can be used to navigate to given url in selenium webdriver in Java.

```
//import the required packages and classes.

import java.io.File;
import java.util.NoSuchElementException;
import java.util.Set;
import java.util.concurrent.TimeUnit;

import org.apache.commons.io.FileUtils;
import org.openqa.selenium.By;
import org.openqa.selenium.JavascriptExecutor;
import org.openqa.selenium.Keys;
import org.openqa.selenium.OutputType;
import org.openqa.selenium.TakesScreenshot;
import org.openqa.selenium.WebDriver;
import org.openqa.selenium.WebElement;
```

```java
import org.openqa.selenium.chrome.ChromeDriver;
import
org.openqa.selenium.firefox.FirefoxDriver;
import org.openqa.selenium.interactions.Action;
import
org.openqa.selenium.interactions.Actions;
import
org.openqa.selenium.support.ui.ExpectedConditio
ns;
import
org.openqa.selenium.support.ui.WebDriverWait;


@SuppressWarnings("unused")
public class OpenGoogle
{

  public static void main(String [] arg)
    {

//set the path of the chrome driver exe file

System.setProperty("webdriver.chrome.driver",
"C:\\Selenuim\\chromedriver2.8.exe");

//create the new instance of the chrome browser
WebDriver driver =  new ChromeDriver();


  try
    {

 //set the implicit and page load time outs

driver.manage().timeouts().implicitlyWait(5,
TimeUnit.SECONDS);
driver.manage().timeouts().pageLoadTimeout(50,T
imeUnit.SECONDS);

//navigate to given url
```

```
driver.get("https://www.google.co.in/preference
s");

//Maximize the browser window
driver.manage().window().maximize();

Thread.sleep(2000);

  }

  catch(Exception e)
  {
 System.out.println("Exception - > " +
e.toString());
  }
 finally
 {
  driver.close();
  driver.quit();
 }
} //main function ends

}//class ends
```

Above code will open chrome browser and navigate
to https://www.google.co.in/preferences

For Firefox Browser

```
//create a new firefox driver object
WebDriver ffdriver =  new FirefoxDriver();
//navigate to google.com
ffdriver.navigate().to("http://www.google.com")
;
```

For Internet Explorer Browser

```
System.setProperty("webdriver.ie.driver",
"C:\\SelenuimProject\\IEDriverServer.exe");
//wb =  new InternetExplorerDriver();
wb.navigate().to("http://www.google.com");
```

You can also use get method to open any website as mentioned below.

```
ffdriver.get("http://www.yahoo.com");
```

7.3 Getting window title

Selenium Java API provides getTitle method which can be used to get the title of the page currently open in the website.

Below example shows how we can get the title of the web page in java using selenium webdriver.

```
//import the required packages and classes.

import java.io.File;
import java.util.NoSuchElementException;
import java.util.Set;
import java.util.concurrent.TimeUnit;

import org.apache.commons.io.FileUtils;
import org.openqa.selenium.By;
import org.openqa.selenium.JavascriptExecutor;
import org.openqa.selenium.Keys;
import org.openqa.selenium.OutputType;
import org.openqa.selenium.TakesScreenshot;
import org.openqa.selenium.WebDriver;
```

```
import org.openqa.selenium.WebElement;
import org.openqa.selenium.chrome.ChromeDriver;
import
org.openqa.selenium.firefox.FirefoxDriver;
import org.openqa.selenium.interactions.Action;
import
org.openqa.selenium.interactions.Actions;
import
org.openqa.selenium.support.ui.ExpectedConditio
ns;
import
org.openqa.selenium.support.ui.WebDriverWait;

@SuppressWarnings("unused")
public class OpenGoogle
{

   public static void main(String [] arg)
   {

//set the path of the chrome driver exe file
System.setProperty("webdriver.chrome.driver",
"C:\\Selenuim\\chromedriver2.8.exe");

//create the new instance of the chrome browser
WebDriver driver =  new ChromeDriver();

 try
 {

driver.manage().timeouts().implicitlyWait(5,
TimeUnit.SECONDS);
driver.manage().timeouts().pageLoadTimeout(50,T
imeUnit.SECONDS);

//navigate to given url
driver.get("https://www.mindtree.com");

//get the title of the home page at
mindetree.com
```

```
String title = driver.getTitle();

Thread.sleep(2000);

 }

 catch(Exception e)
 {
 System.out.println("Exception - > " +
e.toString());
 }
 finally
 {
  driver.close();
  driver.quit();
 }
} //main function ends

}//class ends
```

Please note that same code works for other browsers like IE, Chrome, SAFARI etc

7.4 Maximizing browser window

You can use below code to maximize the browser window in selenium.

```
//import the required packages and classes.

import java.io.File;
import java.util.NoSuchElementException;
import java.util.Set;
import java.util.concurrent.TimeUnit;

import org.apache.commons.io.FileUtils;
import org.openqa.selenium.By;
```

```java
import org.openqa.selenium.JavascriptExecutor;
import org.openqa.selenium.Keys;
import org.openqa.selenium.OutputType;
import org.openqa.selenium.TakesScreenshot;
import org.openqa.selenium.WebDriver;
import org.openqa.selenium.WebElement;
import org.openqa.selenium.chrome.ChromeDriver;
import org.openqa.selenium.firefox.FirefoxDriver;
import org.openqa.selenium.interactions.Action;
import org.openqa.selenium.interactions.Actions;
import org.openqa.selenium.support.ui.ExpectedConditions;
import org.openqa.selenium.support.ui.WebDriverWait;


@SuppressWarnings("unused")
public class OpenGoogle
{

  public static void main(String [] arg)
  {

//set the path of the chrome driver exe file

System.setProperty("webdriver.chrome.driver",
"C:\\Selenuim\\chromedriver2.8.exe");

//create the new instance of the chrome browser
WebDriver driver =  new ChromeDriver();


 try
 {

//below code will maximize the browser window.
driver.manage().window().maximize();
```

```
driver.get("http://www.selenium-interview-
questions.blogspot.in");


  Thread.sleep(2000);


  }


  catch(Exception e)
  {
  System.out.println("Exception - > " +
e.toString());
  }
  finally
  {
   driver.close();
   driver.quit();
  }
} //main function ends

}//class ends
```

7.5 Navigate back and forward

You can use below code to navigate back and forward in Selenium.

```
driver.navigate().back();
driver.navigate().forward();
```

7.6 How to get current url

We can get the current url in a browser in Selenium using below code.

```
String currentUrl =   driver.getCurrentUrl();
```

7.7 How to refresh page

You can use below code to refresh the page in Selenium.

```
driver.navigate().refresh();
```

Alternatively, you can refresh the page by pressing F5 key using sendKeys method or Robotium.

7.8 How to get html source code of current page

Below code can be used to get the html source of the current web page in Selenium.

```
String pageSource = driver.getPageSource();
```

7.9 Resizing and moving browser window

To resize the browser window, we can use below line. Dimension constructor takes 2 parameters - Height and width of the window.

```
driver.manage().window().setSize(new
Dimension(100,100));
```

To set the browser window position, you can use below line of code. Point constructor takes 2 parameters - X and

Y co-ordinates of the browser window. Below statement will move the window down by 200 pixel.

```
driver.manage().window().setPosition(new
Point(0,200));
```

To maximize window, you can use below line of code.

```
driver.manage().window().maximize();
```

8.Element identification

8.1 Element Identification methods

Element identification methods are common in all languages like Java, C#.Net etc with some syntactical differences.

We can identify the web elements in selenium web driver using below methods.

1. By Xpath
2. By Css Selectors
3. By Id
4. By Name
5. By Tag Name
6. By Class Name
7. By Linktext
8. By Partial Link text

Out of these methods, xpath and css selector methods are very popular and useful. We can use xpath and css selectors to identify all kinds of elements in the webpage.

We can also identify the elements using Id, Name, Class Name provided that given element is assigned some id, name or class name.

We can also identify the elements using the html tags like table, div, form etc.

For identifying the links, selenium web driver provides 2 additional methods like link text and Partial link text.

Web Element Identification Examples in Java -

```
driver.findElement(By.tagName("TD"));
```

Above method will return the first element with given tag - TD.

Example -

```
WebElement e =
driver.findElement(By.tagName("div"));
```

Above line will get the first element whose tag is div.

To get all div elements, you can use below code

```
List <WebElement> we_collection =
driver.findElements(By.tagName("div"));
```

Please note that to get the single element we use findElement method and
to get the collection of elements we use findElements method

You can also access the element if you know its class name by using below code

```
driver.findElement(By.className("box"));
```

You can access the element if you know its id by using below code

```
driver.findElement(By.id("selenium"));
```

You can also access the element if you know the value of name attribute by using below code

```
driver.findElement(By.name("sagar"));
```

To find the links in web page, there are 2 ways as mentioned below.

```
driver.findElement(By.partialLinkText("news"));
driver.findElement(By.linkText("hello"));
```

If you know the part of the name of link, you can use **By.partialLinkText**
If you know the whole link name, you can use **By.linkText**

You can also access the element if you know its xpath expression by using below code

```
driver.findElement(By.xpath("//table"));
```

You can also access the element if you know its css expression by using below code

```
driver.findElement(By.cssSelector("#kid"));
```

To find all elements you can use below syntax.

```
List<WebElement> cells =
tr.get(1).findElements(By.tagName("td"));
```

Above code will select all TD elements from the webpage.

Please note that some automation engineers use different terminologies for element identification like object identification methods or Selenium locators etc. In UFT, we use object repository to store the objects. In Selenium, we do not have separate file to store the objects or elements. But we can create our custom file which may store information about objects and their locators.

8.2 Check if element really exists on page

Automation testing with Selenium often lands in the situation where you need to check if specific element exists.

We can do it very easily using below lines of code in Java.

```
if (driver.findElements(By.id("abc")).size() !=
0)
    System.out.println("Element is present");
else    System.out.println("Element is not
present");
```

In other language APIs like Java or Python, you can use similar method to check if element exists or not.

Please note that if you use **FindElement** method, **NoSuchElementException** will be thrown

8.3 Check if pop up really exists on page

You can use below code to check if Alert pop up (Modal Dialog) is open on the web page or not.

```
try
{
    driver.switchTo().alert();

    // Alert exists and we switched to it
}
catch (NoAlertPresentException exception)
{

    //this block will be executed in case
alert is not present
}
```

You will need this code in scenario where you can not predict the presence of the Pop up Alert.

9. Element operations

9.1 Clicking buttons, links or any other web elements

We can click any link or web button or any web element in a webpage by using click() method provided in Selenium webdriver API in JAVA.

Example -

```
WebElement e =
driver.findElement(By.id("myid"));
e.click();
```

Above code will click on the element (link/button etc) whose id attribute value is - myid

Complete Example to click on button or link using Selenium Webdriver in Java

Below example shows how we can click on any element in selenium webdriver in Java.

```
//import the required packages and classes.

import java.io.File;
import java.util.NoSuchElementException;
import java.util.Set;
import java.util.concurrent.TimeUnit;

import org.apache.commons.io.FileUtils;
import org.openqa.selenium.By;
import org.openqa.selenium.JavascriptExecutor;
```

```java
import org.openqa.selenium.Keys;
import org.openqa.selenium.OutputType;
import org.openqa.selenium.TakesScreenshot;
import org.openqa.selenium.WebDriver;
import org.openqa.selenium.WebElement;
import org.openqa.selenium.chrome.ChromeDriver;
import
org.openqa.selenium.firefox.FirefoxDriver;
import org.openqa.selenium.interactions.Action;
import
org.openqa.selenium.interactions.Actions;
import
org.openqa.selenium.support.ui.ExpectedConditio
ns;
import
org.openqa.selenium.support.ui.WebDriverWait;

@SuppressWarnings("unused")
public class OpenGoogle {

public static void main(String [] arg)
{

//set the path of the chrome driver exe file

System.setProperty("webdriver.chrome.driver",
"C:\\Selenuim\\chromedriver2.8.exe");

//create the new instance of the chrome browser
WebDriver driver =  new ChromeDriver();

 try
 {

//set the implicit and page load time outs

driver.manage().timeouts().implicitlyWait(5,
TimeUnit.SECONDS);
driver.manage().timeouts().pageLoadTimeout(50,T
imeUnit.SECONDS);
```

```
//navigate to given url
driver.get("https://www.google.co.in/preference
s");

//Maximize the browser window
driver.manage().window().maximize();

//identify the button or link element using id
WebElement e =
driver.findElement(By.id("myid"));

//enter value in the editbox
e.click()


Thread.sleep(2000);

}

  catch(Exception e)
  {
  System.out.println("Exception - > " +
e.toString());
  }
  finally
  {
   driver.close();
   driver.quit();
  }
} //main function ends

}//class ends
```

Above code will click the element with id attribute value is
- myid

We can also click on the web element by using java script code as mentioned below.

```
((JavascriptExecutor)
driver).executeScript("arguments[0].click()",e)
;
```

9.2 Entering data in text boxes

We can enter the data in editbox or input box in a webpage by using sendKeys method.

```
WebElement e =
driver.findElement(By.id("mainb"));
e.sendKeys("hello")
```

Above code will enter hello in the edit box / text box having id - mainb

Complete Example to enter data in editbox using Selenium Webdriver in Java

Below example shows how we can enter the data in edit box in selenium webdriver in Java.

```
//import the required packages and classes.

import java.io.File;
import java.util.NoSuchElementException;
import java.util.Set;
import java.util.concurrent.TimeUnit;

import org.apache.commons.io.FileUtils;
import org.openqa.selenium.By;
import org.openqa.selenium.JavascriptExecutor;
```

```java
import org.openqa.selenium.Keys;
import org.openqa.selenium.OutputType;
import org.openqa.selenium.TakesScreenshot;
import org.openqa.selenium.WebDriver;
import org.openqa.selenium.WebElement;
import org.openqa.selenium.chrome.ChromeDriver;
import org.openqa.selenium.firefox.FirefoxDriver;
import org.openqa.selenium.interactions.Action;
import org.openqa.selenium.interactions.Actions;
import org.openqa.selenium.support.ui.ExpectedConditions;
import org.openqa.selenium.support.ui.WebDriverWait;


//import com.sun.jna.platform.FileUtils;

@SuppressWarnings("unused")
public class OpenGoogle
{

  public static void main(String [] arg)
  {

//set the path of the chrome driver exe file

System.setProperty("webdriver.chrome.driver",
"C:\\Selenuim\\chromedriver2.8.exe");

//create the new instance of the chrome browser
WebDriver driver =  new ChromeDriver();

  try
  {

//set the implicit and page load time outs
```

```
driver.manage().timeouts().implicitlyWait(5,
TimeUnit.SECONDS);
driver.manage().timeouts().pageLoadTimeout(50,T
imeUnit.SECONDS);

//navigate to given url
driver.get("https://www.google.co.in/preference
s");

//Maximize the browser window
driver.manage().window().maximize();

//identify the edit box element using id
WebElement e =
driver.findElement(By.id("myid"));

//enter value in the editbox
e.sendKeys("hello")

Thread.sleep(2000);
}

 catch(Exception e)
 {
 System.out.println("Exception - > " +
e.toString());
 }
 finally
 {
  driver.close();
  driver.quit();
 }
} //main function ends

}//class ends
```

Above code will enter hello in the edit box whose id
attribute value is - myid

9.3 Selecting the value from the web list

Example - We can select the value from the drop down by using 3 methods.

1. selectByVisibleText - select by the text displayed in drop down
2. selectByIndex - select by index of option in drop down
3. selectByValue - select by value of option in drop down

Consider below code. Suppose you want to select the first option in the combo box.

```
<select id="44">
  <option value="1">xyz</option>
  <option value="2">abc</option>
  <option value="3">pqr</option>
</select>
```

Complete Example in Selenium Webdriver in Java

Below Java example shows how you can select the first value from the combo box using selenium webdriver.

```
//import the required packages and classes.

import java.io.File;
import java.util.NoSuchElementException;
import java.util.Set;
import java.util.concurrent.TimeUnit;

import org.apache.commons.io.FileUtils;
import org.openqa.selenium.By;
import org.openqa.selenium.JavascriptExecutor;
```

```java
import org.openqa.selenium.Keys;
import org.openqa.selenium.OutputType;
import org.openqa.selenium.TakesScreenshot;
import org.openqa.selenium.WebDriver;
import org.openqa.selenium.WebElement;
import org.openqa.selenium.chrome.ChromeDriver;
import org.openqa.selenium.firefox.FirefoxDriver;
import org.openqa.selenium.interactions.Action;
import org.openqa.selenium.interactions.Actions;
import org.openqa.selenium.support.ui.ExpectedConditio
ns;
import org.openqa.selenium.support.ui.WebDriverWait;


@SuppressWarnings("unused")
public class OpenGoogle
{

  public static void main(String [] arg)
  {

//set the path of the chrome driver exe file

System.setProperty("webdriver.chrome.driver",
"C:\\Selenuim\\chromedriver2.8.exe");

//create the new instance of the chrome browser
WebDriver driver =  new ChromeDriver();

  try
  {

//set the implicit and page load time outs

driver.manage().timeouts().implicitlyWait(5,
TimeUnit.SECONDS);
```

```
driver.manage().timeouts().pageLoadTimeout(50,T
imeUnit.SECONDS);

//navigate to given url
driver.get("https://www.google.co.in/preference
s");

//Maximize the browser window
driver.manage().window().maximize();

WebElement e = driver.findElement(By.id("44"));
Select selectElement=new Select(e);

// both of the below statements will select
first option in the weblist
selectElement.selectByVisibleText("xyz");

selectElement.selectByValue("1");

  Thread.sleep(2000);

  }

  catch(Exception e)
  {
  System.out.println("Exception - > " +
e.toString());
  }
  finally
  {
   driver.close();
   driver.quit();
  }
} //main function ends

}//class ends
```

9.4 Reading all items or values from the drop down box

Below code shows how we can print the text of all options in drop down box in Selenium in Java.

```java
package seleniumtest;

//import the required classes
import java.text.SimpleDateFormat;
import java.util.Date;
import java.util.List;
import java.util.Set;
import java.util.concurrent.TimeUnit;

import org.openqa.selenium.By;
import org.openqa.selenium.WebDriver;
import org.openqa.selenium.WebElement;
import org.openqa.selenium.ie.InternetExplorerDriver;
import org.openqa.selenium.support.ui.Select;

public class ElementIdentification
{

  public static void main(String[] args)
  {

      WebDriver driver =null;
      //set the driver path

System.setProperty("webdriver.chrome.driver",
"F:\\selenium\\csharp\\chromedriver.exe");

      System.setProperty("webdriver.ie.driver",
"F:\\selenium\\IEDriverServer_Win32_2.43.0\\IED
riverServer.exe");
```

```
    driver = new InternetExplorerDriver();

    //set the timeouts for page load and all
elements

driver.manage().timeouts().pageLoadTimeout(60,
TimeUnit.SECONDS);

driver.manage().timeouts().implicitlyWait(20,
TimeUnit.SECONDS);


    try
    {

     //open the given web page


driver.get("http://register.rediff.com/commonre
g/index.php");

//driver.get("file:///F:/selenium/selenium-
blog.html");

    //Maximise the browser window
    driver.manage().window().maximize();


//System.out.println(driver.getPageSource());

    System.out.println(driver.getTitle());


    System.out.println(driver.getCurrentUrl());

    WebElement y =
driver.findElement(By.id("date_day"));
```

```
    Select p = new Select(y);
    p.selectByVisibleText("11");
    String z =
p.getFirstSelectedOption().getAttribute("value"
);
    System.out.println(z);

    List <WebElement> k = p.getOptions();
    //Code to print the text values of the
options in list box
    for(int i=0; i<k.size();i++)
     System.out.println(k.get(i).getText());



    //wait for 2 seconds
    Thread.sleep(2000);
    }catch(Exception e){

    //print exception if any
    System.out.println(e.getMessage() );
    e.printStackTrace();
  }
   finally
   {

   //close the driver
   driver.close();
   //quit the driver.
   driver.quit();
   }
 }
}
```

9.5 Selecting the check box

You can see if checkbox is checked or not using below code.

Example -

```
//import the required packages and classes.

import java.io.File;
import java.util.NoSuchElementException;
import java.util.Set;
import java.util.concurrent.TimeUnit;
import org.apache.commons.io.FileUtils;
import org.openqa.selenium.By;
import org.openqa.selenium.JavascriptExecutor;
import org.openqa.selenium.Keys;
import org.openqa.selenium.OutputType;
import org.openqa.selenium.TakesScreenshot;
import org.openqa.selenium.WebDriver;
import org.openqa.selenium.WebElement;
import org.openqa.selenium.chrome.ChromeDriver;
import
org.openqa.selenium.firefox.FirefoxDriver;
import org.openqa.selenium.interactions.Action;
import
org.openqa.selenium.interactions.Actions;
import
org.openqa.selenium.support.ui.ExpectedConditio
ns;
import
org.openqa.selenium.support.ui.WebDriverWait;

@SuppressWarnings("unused")
public class OpenGoogle
{

  public static void main(String [] arg)
  {
```

```
//set the path of the chrome driver exe file

System.setProperty("webdriver.chrome.driver",
"C:\\Selenuim\\chromedriver2.8.exe");

//create the new instance of the chrome browser
WebDriver driver =  new ChromeDriver();


 try
 {

 //set the implicit and page load time outs

driver.manage().timeouts().implicitlyWait(5,
TimeUnit.SECONDS);
driver.manage().timeouts().pageLoadTimeout(50,T
imeUnit.SECONDS);

//navigate to given url
driver.get("https://www.google.co.in/preference
s");

//Maximize the browser window
driver.manage().window().maximize();


boolean x  =
driver.findElement(By.id("myid")).isSelected();

//if check box is not selected, select it using
click method.
if (x == false)
driver.findElement(By.id("myid")).click();

//This is how you can check the checkbox.

//Using same logic, you can uncheck or deselect
the checkbox as displayed below.
```

```java
boolean x  =
driver.findElement(By.id("myid")).isSelected();

if (x == true)
driver.findElement(By.id("myid")).click();

Thread.sleep(2000);

 }

 catch(Exception e)
 {
 System.out.println("Exception - > " +
e.toString());
 }
 finally
 {
  driver.close();
  driver.quit();
 }
} //main function ends

}//class ends
```

9.6 get the value selected in list box

Example - Below example demonstrates how we can select the value from the combo box on the web page using selenium webdriver.

```java
//import the required packages and classes.

import java.io.File;
import java.util.NoSuchElementException;
import java.util.Set;
import java.util.concurrent.TimeUnit;

import org.apache.commons.io.FileUtils;
import org.openqa.selenium.By;
import org.openqa.selenium.JavascriptExecutor;
import org.openqa.selenium.Keys;
import org.openqa.selenium.OutputType;
import org.openqa.selenium.TakesScreenshot;
import org.openqa.selenium.WebDriver;
import org.openqa.selenium.WebElement;
import org.openqa.selenium.chrome.ChromeDriver;
import org.openqa.selenium.firefox.FirefoxDriver;
import org.openqa.selenium.interactions.Action;
import org.openqa.selenium.interactions.Actions;
import org.openqa.selenium.support.ui.ExpectedConditions;
import org.openqa.selenium.support.ui.WebDriverWait;

@SuppressWarnings("unused")
public class OpenGoogle
{

  public static void main(String [] arg)
  {
```

```
//set the path of the chrome driver exe file

System.setProperty("webdriver.chrome.driver",
"C:\\Selenuim\\chromedriver2.8.exe");

//create the new instance of the chrome browser
WebDriver driver =  new ChromeDriver();


try{

//set the implicit and page load time outs

driver.manage().timeouts().implicitlyWait(5,
TimeUnit.SECONDS);
driver.manage().timeouts().pageLoadTimeout(50,T
imeUnit.SECONDS);

//navigate to given url
driver.get("https://www.google.co.in/preference
s");

//Maximize the browser window
driver.manage().window().maximize();

 //identify the element using id
WebElement e =
driver.findElement(By.id("abc"));
Select comboBox = new Select(e);

//get the value selected in drop down using
getAttribute method
value =
comboBox.getFirstSelectedOption().getAttribute(
"value");

System.out.println("Value selected is " + value
);

Thread.sleep(2000);
```

```
}

catch(Exception e)
{
System.out.println("Exception - > " +
e.toString());
}
finally
{
  driver.close();
  driver.quit();
}
} //main function ends

}//class ends
```

9.7 Uploading file

Uploading file using selenium webdriver is very simple. All you have to do is – find the input element having type attribute's value as file and then use sendKeys.

Below code will illustrate how we can upload a file using selenium webdriver in Java.

```java
package abc;
import java.util.concurrent.TimeUnit;
import org.openqa.selenium.By;
import org.openqa.selenium.WebDriver;
import org.openqa.selenium.WebElement;
import org.openqa.selenium.chrome.ChromeDriver;

public class FileUpload
{

 public static void main(String[] args)
 {

  System.setProperty("webdriver.chrome.driver",
  "F:\\chromedriver.exe");
  WebDriver driver =  new ChromeDriver();

  try
  {

    driver.manage().timeouts().setScriptTimeout(
20, TimeUnit.SECONDS);
    driver.manage().timeouts().pageLoadTimeout(5
0, TimeUnit.SECONDS);
    driver.manage().timeouts().implicitlyWait(20
, TimeUnit.SECONDS);

    driver.get("http://www.xyz.com");

    WebElement uploadElement =
driver.findElement(By.id("uploadfile"));

// enter the file path in file input field
uploadElement.sendKeys("C:\\abc.docx");

Thread.sleep(2000);
  }

  catch(Exception ex)
   {
```

```
    System.out.println(ex.toString());
      }
  finally
  {

  driver.close();
  driver.quit();
  }
 }

}
```

9.8 Verify if button is disabled

Selenium web driver provides one method called -
isEnabled which can be used to check if the button is
enabled or disabled in Selenium Webdriver in Java.

```
boolean actualValue = e.isEnabled();
```

above code will check if button e is enabled or disabled. If
it is enabled, actualValue will be true. If it is disabled
actualValue will be false.

**Full example in Java with selenium webdriver to
check if button is disabled**

```
package temp;
import org.openqa.selenium.By;
import org.openqa.selenium.WebDriver;
import org.openqa.selenium.WebElement;
import org.openqa.selenium.chrome.ChromeDriver;
import org.openqa.selenium.support.ui.Select;
```

```java
public class first
{

public static void main(String[] args)
{
  // TODO Auto-generated method stub

System.setProperty("webdriver.chrome.driver", "
C:\\Selenuim\\chromedriver2.3.exe");
WebDriver driver =  new ChromeDriver();

try
{
driver.get("http://register.rediff.com/register
/register.php");

Thread.sleep(2000);
WebElement e =
driver.findElement(By.name("btnemail"));

boolean actualValue = e.isEnabled();

if (actualValue)
      System.out.println("Button is enabled");
else
      System.out.println("Button is
disabled");

Thread.sleep(2000);

}

catch(Exception ex)
{
      System.out.println("Exception " +
ex.getMessage());
}
 finally
  {
```

```
        driver.close();
        driver.quit();
   }
  }

}
```

Please note that we can check the disable property of all kinds of elements like button, checkbox, radiobutton, checkbox, combobox in similar way
using **isEnabled** method in Java using selenium webdriver.

9.9 Verify if button is enabled

Selenium web driver provides one method called - isEnabled which can be used to check if the button is enabled or not in Seleium Webdriver in Java.

```
boolean actualValue = e.isEnabled();
```

above code will check if button e is enabled or not. If it is enabled, actualValue will be true otherwise it will be false.

Full example in Java with selenium webdriver

```
package temp;
import org.openqa.selenium.By;
import org.openqa.selenium.WebDriver;
import org.openqa.selenium.WebElement;
import org.openqa.selenium.chrome.ChromeDriver;
import org.openqa.selenium.support.ui.Select;


public class first
{
public static void main(String[] args)
{
```

```
    // TODO Auto-generated method stub

System.setProperty("webdriver.chrome.driver", "
C:\\Selenuim\\chromedriver2.3.exe");
WebDriver driver =  new ChromeDriver();
try
{
driver.get("http://register.rediff.com/register
/register.php");


Thread.sleep(2000);
WebElement e =
driver.findElement(By.name("btnemail"));


boolean actualValue = e.isEnabled();


if (actualValue)
        System.out.println("Button is enabled");
else
        System.out.println("Button is not
enabled");

Thread.sleep(2000);
}
catch(Exception ex)
 {
   System.out.println("Exception " +
ex.getMessage());
 }
   finally
   {
      driver.close();
      driver.quit();
   }
}


}
```

Please note that we can check the enable and disable property of all kinds of elements like button, checkbox, radiobutton, checkbox, combobox in similar way using **isEnabled** method in Java using selenium webdriver.

9.10 Verify if check box is selected

Selenium web driver provides one method called - isSelected which can be used to check if the checkbox is selected or not in Selenium Webdriver in Java.

```
boolean actualValue = e.isSelected();
```

If checkbox e is selected , above code will return true
Otherwise it will return false

Full example in Java with selenium webdriver

```
package temp;
import org.openqa.selenium.By;
import org.openqa.selenium.WebDriver;
import org.openqa.selenium.WebElement;
import org.openqa.selenium.chrome.ChromeDriver;
import org.openqa.selenium.support.ui.Select;


public class first
{
public static void main(String[] args)
  {
    // TODO Auto-generated method stub


System.setProperty("webdriver.chrome.driver", "
C:\\Selenuim\\chromedriver2.3.exe");
WebDriver driver =  new ChromeDriver();


try
{
```

```
driver.get("http://register.rediff.com/register
/register.php");


Thread.sleep(2000);
WebElement e =
driver.findElement(By.name("chkemail"));


boolean actualValue = e.isSelected();


if (actualValue)
        System.out.println("Checkbox is
selected");
else
        System.out.println("Checkbox is not
selected");

Thread.sleep(2000);
}
  catch(Exception ex)
  {
        System.out.println("Exception " +
ex.getMessage());
  }
  finally
   {
     driver.close();
     driver.quit();
   }
 }
}
```

Thus we can verify if the checkbox is selected or not using **isSelected** method in Java using selenium webdriver.

9.11 Verify if radio button is selected

Selenium web driver provides one method called - isSelected which can be used to check if the radio button is selected or not in Selenium Webdriver in Java.

```
boolean actualValue = e.isSelected();
```

If radio button is selected , above code will return true Otherwise it will return false

Full example in Java with selenium webdriver

```java
package temp;
import org.openqa.selenium.By;
import org.openqa.selenium.WebDriver;
import org.openqa.selenium.WebElement;
import org.openqa.selenium.chrome.ChromeDriver;
import org.openqa.selenium.support.ui.Select;


public class first
{


public static void main(String[] args)
 {
    // TODO Auto-generated method stub


System.setProperty("webdriver.chrome.driver", "
C:\\Selenuim\\chromedriver2.3.exe");
WebDriver driver =  new ChromeDriver();


    try
    {
driver.get("http://register.rediff.com/register
/register.php");


Thread.sleep(2000);
```

```
WebElement e =
driver.findElement(By.name("gender"));


boolean actualValue = e.isSelected();


if (actualValue)
        System.out.println("Radio Button is
selected");
else
        System.out.println("Radio Button is not
selected");

Thread.sleep(2000);
   }
    catch(Exception ex)
     {
        System.out.println("Exception " +
ex.getMessage());
     }
     finally
     {
       driver.close();
       driver.quit();
     }
   }
}
```

Thus we can verify if the radio button is selected or not using **isSelected** method in Java using selenium webdriver.

9.12 Verify if element is displayed on web page

Selenium webdriver provides one method called - isDisplayed which can be used to check if any element like button, checkbox, link etc is displayed or not on web page in Selenium Webdriver in Java.

```
boolean actualValue = e.isDisplayed();
```

above code will check if button e is displayed or not. If it is displayed, actualValue will be true otherwise it will be false.

Full example in Java with selenium webdriver

```
package temp;
import org.openqa.selenium.By;
import org.openqa.selenium.WebDriver;
import org.openqa.selenium.WebElement;
import org.openqa.selenium.chrome.ChromeDriver;
import org.openqa.selenium.support.ui.Select;


public class first
 {


public static void main(String[] args)
  {
    // TODO Auto-generated method stub


System.setProperty("webdriver.chrome.driver", "
C:\\Selenuim\\chromedriver2.3.exe");
WebDriver driver =  new ChromeDriver();


  try
  {
driver.get("http://register.rediff.com/register
/register.php");
Thread.sleep(2000);
```

```
WebElement e =
driver.findElement(By.name("btnemail"));

boolean actualValue = e.isDisplayed();

if (actualValue)
        System.out.println("Button is
displayed");
else
        System.out.println("Button is not
displayed");

Thread.sleep(2000);


  }
  catch(Exception ex)
  {
     System.out.println("Exception " +
ex.getMessage());
  }
  finally
  {
    driver.close();
    driver.quit();
  }
 }
}
```

Please note that we can verify if all elements are displayed
or not like button, checkbox, radiobutton, checkbox,
combobox in similar way using **isDisplayed** method in Java
using selenium webdriver.

9.13 Reading any attribute value

Selenium webdriver provides one method called - **getAttribute()** which can be used to read the value of any web element's attribute in Selenium Webdriver in Java.

```
String actualValue = c.getAttribute("value");
```

above code will return the value of the attribute - value of the webelement c in selenium webdriver.

Full example in Java with selenium webdriver

```java
package temp;
import org.openqa.selenium.By;
import org.openqa.selenium.WebDriver;
import org.openqa.selenium.WebElement;
import org.openqa.selenium.chrome.ChromeDriver;
import org.openqa.selenium.support.ui.Select;


public class first
{
public static void main(String[] args)
  {
    // TODO Auto-generated method stub


System.setProperty("webdriver.chrome.driver", "
C:\\Selenuim\\chromedriver2.3.exe");
WebDriver driver =  new ChromeDriver();


    try
    {
driver.get("http://register.rediff.com/register
/register.php");


Thread.sleep(2000);
WebElement e =
driver.findElement(By.tagName("td"));
```

```
String actualValue = e.getAttribute("value");


        System.out.println("value of the e ->
" + actualValue);

Thread.sleep(2000);
      }


   catch(Exception ex)
   {
       System.out.println("Exception " +
ex.getMessage());
      }
   finally
    {
       driver.close();
       driver.quit();
      }
    }
}
```

Please note that we can get the value of attribute of all other web elements like button, checkbox, radiobutton, checkbox, combobox in similar way
using **getAttribute** method in Java using selenium webdriver.

9.14 Reading CSS value

Selenium webdriver provides one method called - **getCssValue()** which can be used to read the value of any web element's style attribute in Selenium Webdriver in Java.

```
String actualValue = c.getCssValue("width");
```

above code will return the value of the style attribute - width of the webelement c in selenium webdriver.

Full example in Java with selenium webdriver

```
package temp;
import org.openqa.selenium.By;
import org.openqa.selenium.WebDriver;
import org.openqa.selenium.WebElement;
import org.openqa.selenium.chrome.ChromeDriver;
import org.openqa.selenium.support.ui.Select;


public class first
{
public static void main(String[] args)
  {
    // TODO Auto-generated method stub


System.setProperty("webdriver.chrome.driver", "
C:\\Selenuim\\chromedriver2.3.exe");
WebDriver driver =  new ChromeDriver();


    try
    {
driver.get("http://register.rediff.com/register
/register.php");


Thread.sleep(2000);
WebElement e =
driver.findElement(By.tagName("td"));


String actualValue = e.getCssValue("width");


System.out.println("width - of the
webelement  e is -> " + actualValue);


Thread.sleep(2000);
```

```
    }
    catch(Exception ex)
    {
        System.out.println("Exception " +
ex.getMessage());
    }
    finally
    {
      driver.close();
      driver.quit();
    }
  }
}
```

Please note that we can get the value of style attribute of all other web elements like button, checkbox, radiobutton, checkbox, combobox in similar way using **getCssValue** method in Java using selenium webdriver.

9.15 Press Tab key using Selenium

We can press TAB key or any other key in Selenium Web driver by 2 ways in Java.

1. Using Keys.TAB
2. Using Actions

Using Keys.TAB

To use this method, you will have to import below class.
import org.openqa.selenium.Keys;

```
driver.findElement(By.name("name")).sendKeys(Ke
ys.TAB);
```

Using Actions Class

To use this method, you will have to import below classes.
import org.openqa.selenium.interactions.Action;
import org.openqa.selenium.interactions.Actions;

```
Actions action = new Actions(driver);
action.sendKeys(Keys.TAB).build().perform();
```

Complete Example

```java
package temp;
import java.io.File;
import java.util.NoSuchElementException;
import java.util.Set;
import java.util.concurrent.TimeUnit;
import org.apache.commons.io.FileUtils;
import org.openqa.selenium.By;
import org.openqa.selenium.JavascriptExecutor;
import org.openqa.selenium.OutputType;
import org.openqa.selenium.TakesScreenshot;
import org.openqa.selenium.WebDriver;
import org.openqa.selenium.WebElement;
import org.openqa.selenium.chrome.ChromeDriver;
import
org.openqa.selenium.firefox.FirefoxDriver;
import org.openqa.selenium.interactions.Action;
import
org.openqa.selenium.interactions.Actions;
import org.openqa.selenium.Keys;
import
org.openqa.selenium.support.ui.ExpectedConditio
ns;
import
org.openqa.selenium.support.ui.WebDriverWait;

@SuppressWarnings("unused")
```

```
public class SendKey
{

public static void main(String [] arg)

{
System.setProperty("webdriver.chrome.driver",
"C:\\Selenuim\\chromedriver2.8.exe");
WebDriver driver = new ChromeDriver();

try
{

driver.manage().timeouts().implicitlyWait(5,
TimeUnit.SECONDS);

driver.manage().timeouts().pageLoadTimeout(50,T
imeUnit.SECONDS);

driver.get("https://www.google.co.in/preference
s");

driver.manage().window().maximize();

//driver.get("http://register.rediff.com/regist
er/register.php");

Thread.sleep(2000);

WebElement e =
driver.findElement(By.xpath("//div[@id='instant
-radio']/div[3]/span"));
//using Keys.TAB
e.sendKeys(Keys.TAB);

//using Actions

Actions action = new Actions(driver);

action.sendKeys(e,Keys.TAB).build().perform();
```

```
}

catch(Exception e)
{

  System.out.println("Exception - > " +
e.toString());

}

finally
{
  driver.close();
  driver.quit();
}

} //main function ends

}//class ends
```

Please note that we can also press any other key like
ENTER, F1, F2, HOME, ARROW_UP, ESCAPE in same
fashion.

9.16 Press Enter F1 key in Selenium

We can press TAB key or any other key in Selenium Web driver by 2 ways in C#.Net using Keys class

OpenQA.Selenium.Keys

Complete Example in C#.Net is given below to press enter key.

```
using System;
using System.Collections.Generic;
using System.Linq;
using System.Text;
using System.Threading;
using OpenQA.Selenium;
using OpenQA.Selenium.Keys;
using OpenQA.Selenium.Firefox;
using OpenQA.Selenium.Chrome;
using OpenQA.Selenium.IE;
//for SelectElement
using OpenQA.Selenium.Support.UI;
using System.Collections.ObjectModel;
//for events - Actions
using OpenQA.Selenium.Interactions;
//screenshot
using System.Drawing.Imaging;

namespace Abc
{
    class Program
    {
        static void Main(string[] args)
        {
            //IWebDriver x = new
InternetExplorerDriver(@"F:\selenium\csharp");
            //IWebDriver x = new
FirefoxDriver();
            IWebDriver driver=null;
          try
```

```
            {
                driver
= new ChromeDriver(@"F:\selenium\csharp");
                driver.Url
= "http://register.rediff.com/register/register
.php";

                driver.Manage().Timeouts().Impl
icitlyWait(TimeSpan.FromSeconds(20));
                driver.Manage().Timeouts().SetP
ageLoadTimeout(TimeSpan.FromSeconds(50));
                driver.Manage().Window.Maximize
();
                driver.Navigate();

                IWebElement e =
driver.FindElement(By.Name("showdetail"))
                e.SendKeys(Keys.Enter)
            }
            catch(Exception e)
            {
                Console.WriteLine("Exception
....*********"+e.ToString());
            }

            finally
            {
            Thread.Sleep(2000);
            driver.Quit();
            Console.ReadLine();
            }
        }
    }
}
```

Please note that we can also press any other key like F1, F2, HOME, ARROW_UP, ESCAPE in same fashion.

9.17 Press control, shift and delete keys in Selenium

We can use below code to press control, delete and shift keys in Selenium.

```
driver.findElement(By.id("abc")).sendKeys(Keys.
CONTROL + "a");

driver.findElement(By.id("abc")).sendKeys(Keys.
DELETE);
 String keys = Keys.chord(Keys.ALT,
Keys.SHIFT,"p");

driver.findElement(By.id("abc")).sendKeys(keys)
;

driver.findElement(By.name("name")).sendKeys(Ke
ys.TAB);
```

9.18 Clearing data from text box using JavaScriptExecutor

Sometimes, clear method does not work. It does not clear the data from text box. In those situations, we can use Java Script to clear the data.
Below line clears the data from edit box.

```
((JavascriptExecutor)
driver).executeScript("arguments[0].value
='';", element);
```

Note that second parameter is the name of Web Element (Text box).

9.19 Verify if any text is present

We can use below xpath selector to verify if the text is present on a web page in Selenium.

```
//*[contains(text(),'text data')]
```

Note that above xpath will identify text wrapped in any element like div, span etc.
Only condition is that text should be inside one specific tag.

10. Synchronization

10.1 Adding synchronization points

We can add synchronization points in Selenium using 3 ways as mentioned below.
1. Page Load Synchronization
2. Element Synchronization
3. Specific condition synchronization

Page Load Synchronization

We can set the default page navigation timeout. Below statement will set the navigation timeout as 50. This means that selenium script will wait for maximum 50 seconds for page to load. If page does not load within 50 seconds, it will throw an exception.

```
driver.manage().timeouts().pageLoadTimeout(50,T
imeUnit.SECONDS);
```

Element Synchronization

We can set the default element existance timeout. Below statement will set the default object synchronization timeout as 20. This means that selenium script will wait for maximum 20 seconds for element to exist. If Web element does not exist within 20 seconds, it will throw an exception.

```
driver.manage().timeouts().implicitlyWait(20,
TimeUnit.SECONDS);
```

Synchronization based upon specific condition

We can also instruct selenium to wait until element is in expected condition.

To use this kind of synchronization, you will have to
import WebDriverWait class using below statement.

```
import
org.openqa.selenium.support.ui.WebDriverWait;

WebDriverWait w = new WebDriverWait(driver,20);
w.ignoring(NoSuchElementException.class);
WebElement P = null;

//below statement will wait until element
becomes visible
P=w.until(ExpectedConditions.visibilityOfElemen
tLocated(By.id("x")));

//below statement will wait until element
becomes clickable.
p=
w.until(ExpectedConditions.elementToBeClickable
(By.id("ss")));
```

Sample example of Synchronization in selenium in Java

```
//import the required packages and classes.

import java.io.File;
import java.util.NoSuchElementException;
import java.util.Set;
import java.util.concurrent.TimeUnit;

import org.apache.commons.io.FileUtils;
import org.openqa.selenium.By;
import org.openqa.selenium.JavascriptExecutor;
import org.openqa.selenium.Keys;
import org.openqa.selenium.OutputType;
import org.openqa.selenium.TakesScreenshot;
import org.openqa.selenium.WebDriver;
import org.openqa.selenium.WebElement;
```

```
import org.openqa.selenium.chrome.ChromeDriver;
import
org.openqa.selenium.firefox.FirefoxDriver;
import org.openqa.selenium.interactions.Action;
import
org.openqa.selenium.interactions.Actions;
import
org.openqa.selenium.support.ui.ExpectedConditio
ns;
import
org.openqa.selenium.support.ui.WebDriverWait;


@SuppressWarnings("unused")
public class OpenGoogle
{

public static void main(String [] arg)
{

//set the path of the chrome driver exe file

System.setProperty("webdriver.chrome.driver",
"C:\\Selenuim\\chromedriver2.8.exe");

//create the new instance of the chrome browser
WebDriver driver =  new ChromeDriver();


  try
   {

   //set the implicit wait time out to 20
seconds.
  driver.manage().timeouts().implicitlyWait(20,
TimeUnit.SECONDS);

//set the page load timeout to 50 seconds.
driver.manage().timeouts().pageLoadTimeout(50,T
imeUnit.SECONDS);
```

```
//navigate to given url
driver.get("https://www.google.co.in");

//Maximize the browser window
driver.manage().window().maximize();

Thread.sleep(2000);

 }

 catch(Exception e)
  {
 System.out.println("Exception - > " +
e.toString());
  }
 finally
 {
  driver.close();
  driver.quit();
 }
} //main function ends

}//class ends
```

Explicit Synchronization

We can insert explicit synchronization points in the script
using WebDriverWait class. Please remember that you
have to import this class before you use it.

```
import
org.openqa.selenium.support.ui.WebDriverWait;

import
org.openqa.selenium.support.ui.ExpectedConditio
ns;
```

We can instruct selenium to wait until specific element is in expected condition. For example – in below code, code will wait until element with id – x becomes visible.

```
//create WebDriverWait object

WebDriverWait w = new WebDriverWait(driver,20);

//add exceptions to ignore
w.ignoring(NoSuchElementException.class);

WebElement P = null;
//below statement will wait until element
becomes visible

P=w.until(ExpectedConditions.visibilityOfElemen
tLocated(By.id("x")));

//below statement will wait until element
becomes clickable.
p=
w.until(ExpectedConditions.elementToBeClickable
(By.id("ss")));
```

10.2 How to avoid Thread.Sleep in Selenium

I have seen many automation engineers using fixed wait (sleep) statements in selenium or any other automation tool. My personal opinion says that we should never use fixed wait statements in the code as it will slow down the test execution unnecessarily. Sometimes fixed sleep statements might solve your problems. Let us say you added a statement to wait for 5 seconds and the code is working fine today but what will happen if in next release 5 second wait is not sufficient. We never know. This is a risky approach and a bad coding practice.

When the test cases are failing due to synchronization issues, we often tend to blame the network speed, application latency or browser limitations. But that is not the case at all times. You can avoid these wait statements in your code by adopting standard coding practices as mentioned below.

1. **Use WebDriverWait and ExpectedConditions class -** I recommend that we should use these classes whenever we think that test might fail due to synchronization issue. With the help of these classes we can make selenium webdriver wait until some condition is satisfied like specific element getting enabled or displayed.

2. **While switching to the new browser window,** ensure that the web document is really loaded into the window before trying to perform any operation. In one of the projects, I faced the issue in which I was trying to switch to the window. But due to the latency, test was failing unpredictably. I ensured that count of window handles is 2. But still I was facing the issue in random runs. I used 10 second fix wait but still problem persisted. I kept on increasing the sleep time but finally I realized that there must be better technique to handle this scenario. Then I used a loop to check that title of the window has changed as per the expected one and then I tried to switch to it. This made my code more robust. This is how I got rid of sleep statements in the code. If you are still not able to switch to the new window, try to switch to the first window and re-switch to the new window.

3. Another scenario where testers often use wait statements is when **selecting the value from the**

drop down. The issue here is - After selecting the value from the drop down box, new web controls or elements are added or removed from the page dynamically. In this situation, sometimes page itself become unresponsive. In this case, we can use custom function which will use loop until we have performed our operation successfully.

10.3 wait until element is displayed

Below example illustrates how to wait until element is displayed in Selenium. Please note that we are not using any wait conditions. Below methods are useful when handling Ajax requests. Ajax gets the data from server and displays it on the page dynamically. So we can use below method until element is displayed.

```java
public boolean waitUntilElementIsDisplayed(By by, int seconds)
{
    if (checkElementExists(by,seconds))
    {
        for (int i=0;i<seconds;i++)
        {
            if
(driver.findElement(by).isDisplayed())
                return true;
            else
                sleep(1000)
        }
        return false;
    }
    else
    {
        return false;
    }
}
```

```java
public boolean checkElementExists(By by, int
seconds)
{
   boolean result=false;
   try
   {
     driver.manage().timeouts().
implicitlyWait(seconds, TimeUnit.SECONDS);
     driver.findElement(by);
     result = true;
   }
  catch
(org.openqa.selenium.NoSuchElementException ex)
   {
      result = false;
   }
   finally
    {
            driver.manage().timeouts().
implicitlyWait(20, TimeUnit.SECONDS);

   }
       return   result;
}
```

10.4 Explicit Wait Conditions

We have below wait conditions in Selenium C# API.

1. Wait until Element exists in page
2. Wait until Element becomes visible on page
3. Wait until page title becomes as expected

Below code waits for element with ID login until it exists. Please note that timeOut variable contains total number of seconds you need to wait.

```
new WebDriverWait(driver,
TimeSpan.FromSeconds(timeOut)).Until(ExpectedCo
nditions.ElementExists((By.Id(login))));
Below code waits for element with ID login
until it gets visible on the page
new WebDriverWait(driver,
TimeSpan.FromSeconds(timeOut)).Until(ExpectedCo
nditions.ElementIsVisible((By.Id(login))));
Below code waits until Page title becomes Yahoo
News
new WebDriverWait(driver,
TimeSpan.FromSeconds(timeOut)).Until(ExpectedCo
nditions.TitleIs("Yahoo News"));
Below code waits until Page title contains News
word new WebDriverWait(driver,
TimeSpan.FromSeconds(timeOut)).Until(ExpectedCo
nditions.TitleContains("News"));
```

In Selenium-Java API, we have more such conditions like wait until the element is refreshed, wait until the element is hidden or wait until text value of the element becomes as expected.

10.5 Wait until element disappears

Below code waits until element disappears in Selenium.

```
public void waitUntilElementDisappear(By by)
{
        for (int i=0;i<=60;i++)
        {
            if (checkElementExists(by))
                sleep(1000)
            else
                break;
        }
}
```

```java
public boolean checkElementExists(By by, int
seconds)
{
        boolean result=false;
        try
        {
            driver.manage().timeouts().

implicitlyWait(seconds, TimeUnit.SECONDS);

            driver.findElement(by);
            result = true;
        }catch
(org.openqa.selenium.NoSuchElementException ex)
        {
            result = false;
        }
        finally
        {
            driver.manage().timeouts().
implicitlyWait(20, TimeUnit.SECONDS);

        }
        return  result;
}
```

10.6 Wait until page title changes

Below method will wait until page title changes to the one passed as parameter in Selenium.

```java
public boolean waitUntilTitleChanges(String
title)
{
        for (int i=0;i<60;i++)
        {
            if
(driver.getTitle().equalsIgnoreCase(title))
                return true
            else
                sleep(1000)
        }
        return false
}
```

10.7 check if element exists

Below code demonstrates how to check if an element exists. The code returns true if element exists. It returns false if element is not found. Please note that code will not throw the exception if element is not present.

```java
public boolean checkElementExists(By by, int
seconds)
{
        boolean result=false;
        try
        {
driver.manage().timeouts().implicitlyWait(secon
ds, TimeUnit.SECONDS);
            driver.findElement(by);
            result = true;
        }catch
(org.openqa.selenium.NoSuchElementException ex)
```

```
        {
            result = false;
        }
        finally
        {

driver.manage().timeouts().implicitlyWait(20,
TimeUnit.SECONDS);

        }
        return    result;
}
```

10.8 Fluent Wait

Fluent wait is used to synchronize the elements in the browser.

Fluent wait allows you to
  1. Specify polling time
  2. Maximum time out
  3. Ignore Exceptions

Consider a scenario wherein you are expecting specific element to appear within 20 seconds. Time to load that element might change from 5 seconds to 20 seconds. In this situation, we can use Fluent Wait as mentioned in below example.

```
@Test
public void testWait()
{
   String driverpath =
System.setProperty("webdriver.chrome.driver", "
C:\\chromedriver.exe");
   driver = new ChromeDriver();
```

```
  driver.manage().timeouts().implicitlyWait(10,
TimeUnit.SECONDS);
  driver.manage().window().maximize();
  driver.get("http://www.softpost.org/selenium-
test-page/");

  Wait wait = new FluentWait(driver)
            .withTimeout(20, TimeUnit.SECONDS)
            .pollingEvery(5, TimeUnit.SECONDS)

.ignoring(NoSuchElementException.class);


  WebElement foo =(WebElement) wait.until(
    new Function<WebDriver, WebElement>() {
    public WebElement apply(WebDriver driver)
    {
    return
driver.findElement(By.xpath("//input[@value='Si
gn up']"));
    }
    }
    );

    driver.close();
    driver.quit();
}
```

Above code will wait until element with
xpath //input[@value='Sign up'] is found. The code will
wait for 20 seconds maximum and throw exception at the
end if element is not found even after 20 seconds.

11. Advanced XPATH and CSS expressions

11.1 Advanced XPATH expressions to identify the elements

As you know we can identify the elements in webpage using various methods as described at the page How to identify elements in webpage in selenium webdriver.

In this article I am going to explain you how we can use xpath to identify the web elements using selenium web driver.

What is xpath in selenium web driver?

xpath is used to find the specific element in the given webpage.
Some of the below examples will demonstrate how we can write the xpath expressions.

Find all elements with tag input	`//input`
Find all input tag element having attribute type = 'hidden'	`//input[@type='hidden']`
Find all input tag element having attribute type = 'hidden' and name attribute = 'ren'	`//input[@type='hidden'][@name='ren']`
Find all input tag element with	`//input[contains(@type,'hid')]`

attribute type containing 'hid'	
Find all input tag element with attribute type starting with 'hid'	`//input[starts-with(@type,'hid')]`
Find all elements having innertext = 'password'	`//*[text()='Password']`
Find all td elements having innertext = 'password'	`//td[text()='Password']`
Find all next siblings of td tag having innertext = 'gender'	`//td[text()='Gender']//following-sibling::*`
Find all elements in the 2nd next sibling of td tag having innertext = 'gender'	`//td[text()='Gender']//following-sibling::*[2]//*`
Find input elements in the 2nd next sibling of td tag having innertext = 'gender'	`//td[text()='Gender']//following-sibling::*[2]//input`
Find the td which contains font element containing the text '12'	`//td[font[contains(text(),'12')]]`
Find all the preceding siblings of the td which contains font element containing the text '12'	`//td[font[contains(text(),'12')]]//preceding-sibling::*`
Find the second td	`//span[text()='Exp`

ancestor of the span element containing text - Exp Date then find the previous td element'	`Date']//ancestor::td[2]//preceding-sibling::td`
Find the first td ancestor of the span element containing text - Exp Date then find the previous td element	`//span[text()='Exp Date']//ancestor::td[1]//preceding-sibling::td`
Find the element containing specific text	`//p[text()[contains(.,'refer')]]`

Logical operators in XPATH - //div[contains(@class,'result-row') and not (contains(@style,'none'))] XPATH contains examples -

1. Handling the quote inside text -
   '//label[contains(text(),"Killer\'s age.")]'

How to use xpath expressions in selenium web driver?

Below example illustrates how we can use xpath expressions in selenium webdriver in Java.

```java
package temp;
import java.util.concurrent.TimeUnit;
import org.openqa.selenium.By;
import org.openqa.selenium.WebDriver;
import org.openqa.selenium.chrome.ChromeDriver;

public class first
{

  public static void main(String[] args)
  {

  System.setProperty("webdriver.chrome.driver",
"C:\\SelenuimProject\\chromedriver.exe");
  WebDriver driver =  new ChromeDriver();

  try
   {

driver.manage().timeouts().pageLoadTimeout(50,
TimeUnit.SECONDS);

driver.manage().timeouts().implicitlyWait(20,
TimeUnit.SECONDS);

driver.get("http://www.register.rediff.com/regi
ster/register.php");

 driver.findElement(By.xpath("//input[starts-
with(@onblur,'field')]")).sendKeys("Sagar
Salunke");

  Thread.sleep(2000);

  }

  catch(Exception ex)
  {
    System.out.println(ex.toString());
```

```
    }
    finally
    {

      driver.close();
      driver.quit();
    }
  }

}
```

I have also got a separate article on finding the relative elements in selenium using xpath. Please check it out.

11.2 Finding relative elements using XPATH

Why finding the relative elements on the page is required?

Well- most of the elements on the webpage can be found using 8 methods then why do we need to find the elements with reference to other elements? There are 2 reasons for this.

2. Sometimes developers do not provide the id for the element making it difficult to find the element. We can find the element by other methods but they will return many elements.
3. Sometimes developers provide the id attributes but their value contains numbers. An if you write xpath or use id having numbers, you are heading to the hell. Because such id values are never reliable and fixed.

How to write XPath expressions that find the relative elements?

We can use following-sibling and preceding-sibling keywords as shown below.

In below image, we have input box with name as "q". Yes, we can use xpath directly in this case. But consider a scenario where you do not have name attribute or the textbox attributes are changing at run time.

In that case, you have a very robust method to find out the textbox using label next to it. There is a rare possibility that label for the textbox will change. So how to write xpath now? We can use following-sibling keyword as shown below. So even if the position of the textbox changes tomorrow, below xpath will be able to find that easily.

```
//td[contains(text(),'Name')]//following-
sibling::td//input
```

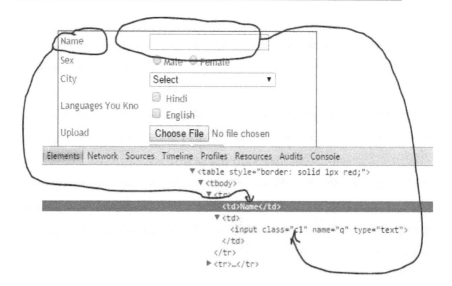

Or other way around, We can find the label of the textbox using below xpath.

```
//input[@name='q']//parent::td//preceding-
sibling::td
```

More xpath expressions are given below.

1. //th[contains(text(),'Example')]//following-sibling::th//text()
2. //span[text()='abc']//parent::td//following-sibling::td
3. //input[contains(@value,'Google')]
4. //span[text()='Contents']//preceding-sibling::input
5. //a[contains(@id,'xyz')]
6. (//span[text()='" + key + "']//parent::td//following-sibling::td//span)[1]
7. //span[text()='Exp Date']//ancestor::td
8. //span[text()='Exp Date']//ancestor::td//preceding-sibling::td
9. //span[text()='Exp Date']//ancestor::td[1]//preceding-sibling::td
10. (//a[contains(@id,'xyz')])[2]

Another example to understand the relative element concept is given below.

On below url, we have a table with update button in each row.
http://www.softpost.org/selenium-test-page/

Imagine that you have a requirement where in you have to click on Update button for a given Employee Id. So if you are asked to click on Update button for Employee with Id 142, it should click on second update button. Ordinary developer will use the copy and paste the XPATH for second button. But we have a problem here. The number of employees are not constant. So if today we have a Employee Id 142 at second row. But after few days, it might move to 6th position or any other position. So we should write the xpath expression in such a way that we should be able to click on the correct Update button even though position of the row changes.

If columns are fixed, you can use below XPATH.

```
//td[contains(text(),'172')]//following-sibling::td[2]//button
```

If columns are not fixed, you can use below XPATH provided that a row has only one button.

```
//td[contains(text(),'172')]//parent::tr//butto
n
```

Both the xpath expressions above, find the button relative to the TD tag that contains Employee Id. So even if Employee Id row changes, Selenium will find the correct button using relative xpath expression.

Employee ID	Email Address	Update information
172	abc@gmail.com	Update
142	pqr@hotmail.com	Update
332	xuz@google.com	Update

```
Q  ☐  Elements  Network  Sources  Timeline  Profiles  Resources  Audits  Console
⊘  ▽  <top frame>  ▼  ☐ Preserve log
> $x("//td[contains(text(),'172')]")
  [ <td>172</td>]
> $x("//td[contains(text(),'172')]//following-sibling::td")
  [ <td>abc@gmail.com</td>, ▶<td>…</td>]
> $x("//td[contains(text(),'172')]//following-sibling::td[2]")
  [ ▶<td>…</td>]
> $x("//td[contains(text(),'172')]//following-sibling::td[2]//button")
  [ <button onclick="alert('you clicked 172');">Update</button>]
> $x("//td[contains(text(),'172')]//parent::tr//button")
  [ <button onclick="alert('you clicked 172');">Update</button>]
> |
```

Above XPATH expressions can also be used to clicking button in specific cell.

11.3 Identify the elements using cssSelector

As you know we can identify the elements in webpage using various methods as described at the page.
I am going to explain you how we can use cssSelectors to identify the web elements using selenium web driver.

What is CssSelector in selenium web driver?

cssSelector is used to find the specific element in the given webpage.

116

Some of the below examples will demonstrate how we can write the cssSelector expressions.

Find all elements with tag input	`input`
Find all input tag element having attribute type = 'hidden'	`input[type='hidden']`
Find all input tag element having attribute type = 'hidden' and name attribute = 'ren'	`input[type='hidden'][name='ren']`
Find all input tag element with attribute type containing 'hid'	`input[type*='hid']`
Find all input tag element with attribute type starting with 'hid'	`input[type^='hid']`
Find all input tag element with attribute type ending with 'den'	`input[type$='den']`

You can find the element containing specific text using below CSS Selector syntax.

```
$("h3:contains('Cloud')")
```

Above css will select the element H3 containing text Cloud

How to use cssSelector expressions in selenium web driver?

Below example illustrates how we can use xpath expressions in selenium webdriver in Java.

```java
package temp;
import java.util.concurrent.TimeUnit;
import org.openqa.selenium.By;
import org.openqa.selenium.WebDriver;
import org.openqa.selenium.chrome.ChromeDriver;

public class first
{

  public static void main(String[] args)
  {

System.setProperty("webdriver.chrome.driver",
"C:\\SelenuimProject\\chromedriver.exe");
    WebDriver driver =  new ChromeDriver();

    try
    {

driver.manage().timeouts().pageLoadTimeout(50,
TimeUnit.SECONDS);

driver.manage().timeouts().implicitlyWait(20,
TimeUnit.SECONDS);

driver.get("http://www.register.rediff.com/regi
ster/register.php");

driver.findElement(By.cssSelector("input[Name='
name']")).sendKeys("Sagar Salunke");

    Thread.sleep(2000);
    }
```

```
  catch(Exception ex)
 {
   System.out.println(ex.toString());
 }
  finally
  {
     driver.close();
     driver.quit();
  }
 }
}
```

12. Working with tables

12.1 How to get the data in table cell

Selenium webdriver provides one method called - getText() which can be used to read the innertext of any web element not just table cell in Selenium Webdriver in Java.

```
String actualValue = c.getText();
```

above code will return the data displayed in cell c in selenium webdriver.

Full example in Java with selenium webdriver

```java
package temp;
import org.openqa.selenium.By;
import org.openqa.selenium.WebDriver;
import org.openqa.selenium.WebElement;
import org.openqa.selenium.chrome.ChromeDriver;
import org.openqa.selenium.support.ui.Select;


public class first
{


public static void main(String[] args)
  {
    // TODO Auto-generated method stub
System.setProperty("webdriver.chrome.driver", "
C:\\Selenuim\\chromedriver2.3.exe");
WebDriver driver =  new ChromeDriver();


try
{
driver.get("http://register.rediff.com/register
/register.php");
```

```
Thread.sleep(2000);
WebElement e =
driver.findElement(By.tagName("td"));
String actualValue = e.getText();
 System.out.println("Text displayed in the
first td -> " + actualValue);

Thread.sleep(2000);
  }
catch(Exception ex)
{
 System.out.println("Exception " +
ex.getMessage());
}
 finally
  {
    driver.close();
    driver.quit();
  }
}
}
```

Please note that we can get the text inside other web elements like button, checkbox, radiobutton, checkbox, combobox in similar way using **getText** method in Java using selenium webdriver.

12.2 Reading data from web tables

Example - Below example in Java demonstrates how we can read the value from the table in web page using selenium webdriver API in Jav.

```java
import java.io.File;
import java.util.NoSuchElementException;
import java.util.Set;
import java.util.concurrent.TimeUnit;

import org.apache.commons.io.FileUtils;
import org.openqa.selenium.By;
import org.openqa.selenium.JavascriptExecutor;
import org.openqa.selenium.Keys;
import org.openqa.selenium.OutputType;
import org.openqa.selenium.TakesScreenshot;
import org.openqa.selenium.WebDriver;
import org.openqa.selenium.WebElement;
import org.openqa.selenium.chrome.ChromeDriver;
import
org.openqa.selenium.firefox.FirefoxDriver;
import org.openqa.selenium.interactions.Action;
import
org.openqa.selenium.interactions.Actions;
import
org.openqa.selenium.support.ui.ExpectedConditio
ns;
import
org.openqa.selenium.support.ui.WebDriverWait;

@SuppressWarnings("unused")
public class OpenGoogle
{

public static void main(String [] arg)
{

//set the path of the chrome driver exe file
```

```
System.setProperty("webdriver.chrome.driver",
"C:\\Selenuim\\chromedriver2.8.exe");

//create the new instance of the chrome browser
WebDriver driver =  new ChromeDriver();

  try
  {

//set the implicit and page load time outs

driver.manage().timeouts().implicitlyWait(5,
TimeUnit.SECONDS);
driver.manage().timeouts().pageLoadTimeout(50,T
imeUnit.SECONDS);

//navigate to given url
driver.get("https://www.google.co.in/preference
s");

//Maximize the browser window
driver.manage().window().maximize();

//get the collection of all rows from the table
List<WebElement> tr =
driver.findElements(By.xpath("//table//tr"));

//get the collection of all cells from the
first row in the table
List<WebElement> cells =
tr.get(1).findElements(By.tagName("td"));

  for (WebElement cell : cells)
  {
    //Here we are printing the contents of
table cells from row 1
    System.out.println( cell.getText()  );
  }
Thread.sleep(2000);
```

```
 }

catch(Exception e)
{
 System.out.println("Exception - > " +
e.toString());
 }
 finally
 {
  driver.close();
  driver.quit();
 }
} //main function ends
}//class ends
```

12.3 Finding total number of rows and columns

We can use below XPATH expressions to find count of rows and columns in a table.

1. //table//th - Find total number of columns in a table. Note that this will only work if all columns are marked using th tag
2. //table//tr - Find total number of rows in a table.
3. //table//tr[1]//td - Find total number of TD tags inside a given table row.

13. Window related things

13.1 Uploading a file

Some times you will have to handle the file upload window using selenium web driver.
Selenium does not provide any such way to handle the window pop ups.

You can use AutoIT script to automate this task. AutoIT is a scripting language for Microsoft windows applications. You will have to download and install AutoIT from this url Download AutoIT

Once downloaded, you can write below code in the script file and invoke that file code just when you need to handle the upload window. Semicolon(;) is used to mark the comments in AutoIT scripts.

```
;below line states Windows controller to wait
for the window with title Open to display.
Whatever is the name of window, you need to
pass it here.

WinWaitActive("Open")

;below line will enter the file location to be
uploaded.
Send("C:\Users\sagar\Documents\onion_fennel_bis
que.jpg")

;finally we need to click on Ok or press enter
to start the upload process.
Send("{ENTER}")
```

Here is the complete example.

```java
package seleniumtest;

//autoIT
//TestNG
//Grid

//import the required classes
import java.text.SimpleDateFormat;
import java.util.Date;
import java.util.Set;
import java.util.concurrent.TimeUnit;

import org.openqa.selenium.By;
import org.openqa.selenium.WebDriver;
import org.openqa.selenium.*;
import org.openqa.selenium.chrome.ChromeDriver;

public  class AutoIT
 {

 public static void main(String[] args)
 {

     WebDriver driver =null;
     //set the driver path

System.setProperty("webdriver.chrome.driver",
 "F:\\selenium\\csharp\\chromedriver.exe");

     System.setProperty("webdriver.ie.driver",
"F:\\selenium\\IEDriverServer_Win32_2.43.0\\IED
riverServer.exe");

     Date dNow = new Date( );


     //create new driver instance
     driver = new ChromeDriver();
```

```
driver.manage().timeouts().pageLoadTimeout(60,
TimeUnit.SECONDS);

driver.manage().timeouts().implicitlyWait(20,
TimeUnit.SECONDS);

   try
   {
      driver.get("https://www.pdftoword.com/");
      driver.findElement(By.id("file-
uploader")).click();
      //please note that below line calls the
AutoIT

 script which will handle the file upload
dialog in google chrome browser.

Also note that we need to provide the path of
exe file which

is created after we compile and build the
AutoIT script.

Runtime.getRuntime().exec("F:\\selenium\\handle
file1.exe");

        //wait for 2 seconds
    Thread.sleep(5000);
   }
  catch(Exception e)
   {

   //print exception if any
   System.out.println(e.getMessage() );
   e.printStackTrace();
   }
    finally
    {
```

```
    //close the driver
    driver.close();
    //quit the driver.
    driver.quit();
    }
  }
}
```

13.2 Auto Downloading file

When you try to download a file from a website in Selenium, window dialog may appear. But Selenium can not handle such native windows. We may use AUTOIT scripts for handling native windows. But that's only possible on Windows OS.

Better solution is to change the driver settings so that file is automatically downloaded to system bypassing the File save dialog.

If you are using Firefox, you can use below code to start the driver with below profile.

```
FirefoxProfile myprofile= new FirefoxProfile();
firefoxProfile.setPreference("browser.download.
manager.showWhenStarting", false);
firefoxProfile.setPreference("browser.download.
dir", "c:\\mydownloadlocation\\xyz");
firefoxProfile.setPreference("browser.helperApp
s.neverAsk.saveToDisk", "application/pdf");
WebDriver driver = new
FirefoxDriver(myprofile);
```

If you are using Chrome driver, you can use below code to skip the download window.

```
        ChromeOptions options = new
ChromeOptions();
        Map<String, Object> prefs = new
HashMap<String, Object>();

prefs.put("download.prompt_for_download",
false);
        prefs.put("download.default_directory",
"path-to-download-directory");
        options.setExperimentalOption("prefs",
prefs);
        WebDriver driver = new
ChromeDriver(options);
```

14. Actions

14.1 Performing drag and drop action

We can drag and drop the elements using Actions class in selenium webdriver in Java.

Below class/Interface must be imported before performing drag and drop in Selenium Webdriver.

import org.openqa.selenium.interactions.Action;
import org.openqa.selenium.interactions.Actions;

```
//create Actions object
Actions builder = new Actions(driver);

//create a chain of actions to move element e1
to e2
Action dragAndDropAction = builder
  .clickAndHold(e1)
  .moveToElement(e2)
  .release(e2)
  .build();


//perform drag and drop action

 dragAndDropAction.perform();
```

14.2 Double click on the web element

We can perform all kinds of mouse and keyboard events in selenium webdriver using Actions interface.

Please note that we need to import below classes/interfaces to perform below operations.

```
import org.openqa.selenium.interactions.Action;
import org.openqa.selenium.interactions.Actions;
```

Java Example to double click on Webelement in Selenium Webdriver

```
package temp;
import java.io.File;
import java.util.concurrent.TimeUnit;

import org.apache.commons.io.FileUtils;
import org.openqa.selenium.By;
import org.openqa.selenium.Keys;
import org.openqa.selenium.OutputType;
import org.openqa.selenium.TakesScreenshot;
import org.openqa.selenium.WebDriver;
import org.openqa.selenium.WebElement;
import org.openqa.selenium.chrome.ChromeDriver;
import org.openqa.selenium.firefox.FirefoxDriver;
import org.openqa.selenium.interactions.Action;
import org.openqa.selenium.interactions.Actions;

@SuppressWarnings("unused")
public class OpenGoogle
{
public static void main(String [] arg)
{
System.setProperty("webdriver.chrome.driver", "
C:\\SelenuimProject\\chromedriver2.8.exe");
WebDriver driver =  new ChromeDriver();
```

```
 try
 {
driver.manage().timeouts().implicitlyWait(20,
TimeUnit.SECONDS);
driver.manage().timeouts().pageLoadTimeout(50,T
imeUnit.SECONDS);

driver.get("http://www.google.com/");

Thread.sleep(3000);

WebElement element =
driver.findElement(By.id("hplogo"));

Actions builder = new Actions(driver);

//build the action chain.
Action doubleclick =
builder.doubleClick(element).build();

//perform the double click action
doubleclick.perform();

Thread.sleep(8000);
}

 catch(Exception e)
 {
   System.out.println("Exception - > " +
e.toString());
 }
 finally
  {
   driver.close();
   driver.quit();
  }
}      //main function ends

}//class ends
```

14.3 Performing mouseover / mouse hover action

Here driver is the WebDriver object and e is the element on which you want to perform mouse over action

Example -

```java
import java.io.File;
import java.util.NoSuchElementException;
import java.util.Set;
import java.util.concurrent.TimeUnit;

import org.apache.commons.io.FileUtils;
import org.openqa.selenium.By;
import org.openqa.selenium.JavascriptExecutor;
import org.openqa.selenium.Keys;
import org.openqa.selenium.OutputType;
import org.openqa.selenium.TakesScreenshot;
import org.openqa.selenium.WebDriver;
import org.openqa.selenium.WebElement;
import org.openqa.selenium.chrome.ChromeDriver;
import org.openqa.selenium.firefox.FirefoxDriver;
import org.openqa.selenium.interactions.Action;
import org.openqa.selenium.interactions.Actions;
import org.openqa.selenium.support.ui.ExpectedConditions;
import org.openqa.selenium.support.ui.WebDriverWait;

@SuppressWarnings("unused")
public class OpenGoogle
{
  public static void main(String [] arg)
  {

//set the path of the chrome driver exe file
```

```java
System.setProperty("webdriver.chrome.driver",
"C:\\Selenuim\\chromedriver2.8.exe");

//create the new instance of the chrome browser
WebDriver driver =  new ChromeDriver();

 try
  {

//set the implicit and page load time outs

driver.manage().timeouts().implicitlyWait(5,
TimeUnit.SECONDS);
driver.manage().timeouts().pageLoadTimeout(50,T
imeUnit.SECONDS);

//navigate to given url
driver.get("https://www.google.co.in/preference
s");

//Maximize the browser window
driver.manage().window().maximize();

//find the element on which you want to mouse
hover
WebElement e =
driver.findElement(By.xpath("//*[@id='Trade_Sum
mary1_1']/table/thead/tr"));

//we can perform complex operations like mouse
over using Actions class
 Actions builder = new Actions(driver);
 Action hoverAction =
builder.moveToElement(e).build();

//perform the mouse over action in selenium
webdriver
 hoverAction.perform();
  Thread.sleep(2000);
```

```
}

catch(Exception e)
  {
    System.out.println("Exception - > " +
e.toString());
  }
  finally
  {
  driver.close();
  driver.quit();
  }
} //main function ends

}//class ends
```

14.4 Opening context menu (right clicking) on webpage

We can perform all kinds of mouse and keyboard events in selenium webdriver using Actions interface.

Please note that we need to import below classes to perform below operations.

```
import org.openqa.selenium.interactions.Action;

import org.openqa.selenium.interactions.Actions;
```

Java Example to right click (opening Context menu) on Webelement in Selenium Webdriver

```java
package temp;
import java.io.File;
import java.util.concurrent.TimeUnit;

import org.apache.commons.io.FileUtils;
import org.openqa.selenium.By;
import org.openqa.selenium.Keys;
import org.openqa.selenium.OutputType;
import org.openqa.selenium.TakesScreenshot;
import org.openqa.selenium.WebDriver;
import org.openqa.selenium.WebElement;
import org.openqa.selenium.chrome.ChromeDriver;
import org.openqa.selenium.firefox.FirefoxDriver;
import org.openqa.selenium.interactions.Action;
import org.openqa.selenium.interactions.Actions;

@SuppressWarnings("unused")
public class OpenGoogle
{
    public static void main(String [] arg)
    {

System.setProperty("webdriver.chrome.driver", "
C:\\SelenuimProject\\chromedriver2.8.exe");
WebDriver driver =  new ChromeDriver();

  try
    {
driver.manage().timeouts().implicitlyWait(20,
TimeUnit.SECONDS);
driver.manage().timeouts().pageLoadTimeout(50,T
imeUnit.SECONDS);

driver.get("http://www.google.com/");

Thread.sleep(3000);

WebElement element =
driver.findElement(By.id("hplogo"));
```

```
Actions builder = new Actions(driver);

//build the action chain.
Action rightclick =
builder.contextClick(element).build();

//perform the action
rightclick.perform();

Thread.sleep(8000);

   }

  catch(Exception e)
   {
     System.out.println("Exception - > " +
e.toString());
   }
    finally
     {
        driver.close();
        driver.quit();
     }
}      //main function ends

}//class ends
```

15. Exceptions in Selenium

15.1 Common Exceptions that might occur

Here is the list of common exceptions in Java in selenium web driver.

1. Element is not clickable at point (x, y).
2. No Such Element - for Frame related issue
3. The driver executable does not exist. Driver executable must be set by the webdriver.ie.driver system property. The path to the driver executable must be set by the webdriver.chrome.driver system property
4. Stale Element Reference - This happens when new element comes in ajax

15.2 Environmental Issues and Exceptions

1. Unexpected error launching Internet Explorer. Protected Mode settings are not the same for all zones You may get below error message when working with Selenium Webdriver and Internet Explorer browser.

Unexpected error launching Internet Explorer. Protected Mode settings are not the same for all zones. Enable Protected Mode must be set to the same value (enabled or disabled) for all zones. (WARNING: The server did not provide any stacktrace information)
Command duration or timeout: 1.43 seconds

To fix above error you need to make below setting in Internet Option -> Security Tab as shown in below image.

Enable Protected Mode must be set to the same value (enabled or disabled) for all zones

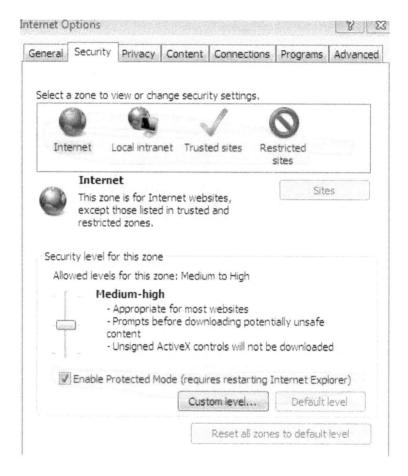

If you have no permission to modify above settings, you can do it using below code.

```
DesiredCapabilities capabilities =
DesiredCapabilities.internetExplorer();
capabilities.setCapability(InternetExplorerDriv
er.
                 INTRODUCE_FLAKINESS_BY_IGNORIN
G_SECURITY_DOMAINS,true);
WebDriver driver = new
InternetExplorerDriver(capabilities);
```

This will launch Internet explorer such that Enable Protected Mode is set to the same value (enabled or disabled) for all zones.

2. The method sendKeys(CharSequence[]) in the type WebElement is not applicable for the arguments (String) You may get below error while working with selenium.

The method sendKeys(CharSequence[]) in the type WebElement is not applicable for the arguments (String)

To fix this error, you will have to change the compiler compliance level of the project to JRE 1.6 or above in Eclipse.
To open below window, you will have to right click on the Java Project folder you are working on.

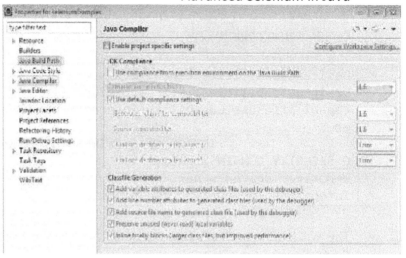

I was getting the sendKeys error when I was using JRE 1.4 compliance level. After changing the compiler compliance level to 1.6, the error was resolved.

3. Timed out receiving message from renderer
You may get exception saying - timeout: Timed out receiving message from renderer when working with Selenium web driver and chrome browser.

I fixed this exception using below statement in Java.

```
driver.manage().timeouts().pageLoadTimeout(60,
TimeUnit.SECONDS);
```

I was getting the exception earlier when the page load time out was 20 seconds. I increased the page load time out to 60 seconds and it started working like a charm.

As a good practise, always make sure that page load time out is at least 60 seconds.

4. Unexpected modal dialog is present in Internet Explorer
When automating the test cases using Selenium WebDriver, we often encounter this error saying "Unexpected Modal Dialog found".

This error usually comes when Selenium Webdriver is not able to perform any operation on the page due to Alert dialog being open on the page.

5. Element is disabled Exception
Sometimes you need to enter data into web controls which are disabled.
But Selenium will throw exceptions saying element is disabled.

So you need to make use of JavaScriptExecutor interface in this scenario.
With JavaScriptExecutor, you can set the data into editbox easily using below syntax.

```
(JavaScriptExecutor
(driver)).executeScript("arguments[0].value =
abc", webelement );
```

6. Unable to switch to new window due to incorrect window handle count
Sometimes, when we click on the link or button, another browser window opens .
Then we can switch to new window using window handle of that window.

Working on one project, I encountered some weird issue. What happened is that after new window was opened, I tried to find the count of window handles. On one machine I was getting the count as 2 while on other I was getting the count as 1. I was using a Internet Explorer 8 browser.

All automation testers were baffled due to the issue. Then Suddenly I realized that this might be happening due to browser settings. I made below change in the security settings of the browser and it started working magically.

I enabled the protected mode for all security zones.

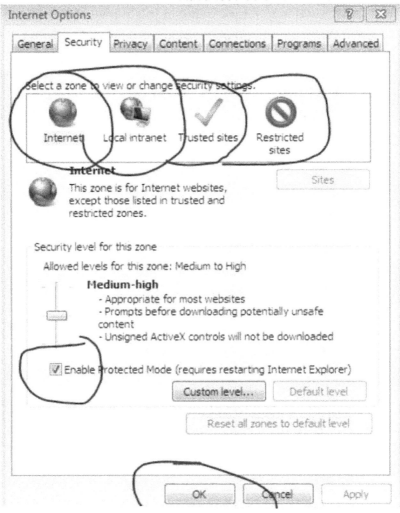

7. StaleElementExeption
8. ElementNotFoundException - unable to find element
9. unable to find element on closed window
10. Unable to find standalone executable
11. Unable to get browser
12. Unable to locate element in Selenium webdriver

13. Unable to locate frame in Selenium webdriver
14. Unable to find element in Selenium webdriver
15. Unable to locate frame in Selenium webdriver
16. Unable to discover open pages in Selenium webdriver
17. No such Element Exception
18. Element is not clickable at this point..Other element would receive the click
19. Driver executable does not exist
20. Element is not currently visible and so may not be interacted with

Synchronization Issues
1. Wait until page loads
2. Wait until Element loads
3. Wait until Element is really able to accept the input

Complex Web Element Issues
1. Unable to select value from the drop down box

Issues related to Selenium Limitations
1. Handling the windows dialog in Selenium

16. Switching context

16.1 Handling multiple browser windows (tabs)

Below code will show you how we can handle pop up windows in selenium in Java.

Selenium webdriver API provides a method called **getWindowHandles()** which can be used to get the handles of open browser windows.

We can switch to the desired window using below syntax.

```
driver.switchTo().window(handle);
```

Sample Java program to handle multiple browser windows is given below

```java
package temp;
import java.io.File;
import java.util.Set;
import java.util.concurrent.TimeUnit;
import org.apache.commons.io.FileUtils;
import org.openqa.selenium.By;
import org.openqa.selenium.Keys;
import org.openqa.selenium.OutputType;
import org.openqa.selenium.TakesScreenshot;
import org.openqa.selenium.WebDriver;
import org.openqa.selenium.WebElement;
import org.openqa.selenium.chrome.ChromeDriver;
import org.openqa.selenium.firefox.FirefoxDriver;
import org.openqa.selenium.interactions.Action;
import org.openqa.selenium.interactions.Actions;

//import com.sun.jna.platform.FileUtils;

@SuppressWarnings("unused")
public class OpenGoogle
{
```

```
  public static void main(String [] arg)
  {

System.setProperty("webdriver.chrome.driver", "
C:\\SelenuimProject\\chromedriver2.8.exe");
WebDriver driver =  new ChromeDriver();

  try
  {
driver.manage().timeouts().implicitlyWait(20,
TimeUnit.SECONDS);
driver.manage().timeouts().pageLoadTimeout(50,T
imeUnit.SECONDS);
//driver.navigate().to("http://www.google.com");

//Please enter your web url here
driver.get("http://www.xyz.com/");

String mainHandle = driver.getWindowHandle();

driver.findElement(By.LinkText("Open New
Window")).click();

//wait while ( driver.getWindowHandles().size() == 1 );

Set<String> HandleSet =
driver.getWindowHandles();
//Switching to the popup window.

for ( String handle : HandleSet )
{
    if(!handle.equals(mainHandle))
    {
        //Switch to newly created window
          driver.switchTo().window(handle);
    }
}

}
```

```
catch(Exception e)
{
   System.out.println("Exception - > " + e.toString());
}
finally
{
   driver.close();
   driver.quit();
}
}      //main function ends

}//class ends
```

16.2 Handling alerts (modal dialogs)

We can handle the alerts very easily in selenium webdriver in Java using switchTo() method.
We can handle alerts using Alert Interface in Java Web Driver.

At first, we need to get the alert reference using below syntax.

```
Alert alert = driver.switchTo().alert()
```

Then we can click on Ok button using below syntax.

```
alert.accept();
```

Then we can click on Cancel button using below syntax.

```
alert.dismiss();
```

To get the text displayed in the alert, you can use getText() method

```
String text = alert.getText();
```

//Sample Java program to handle alert in selenium webdriver

```
package seleniumtest;

import java.util.concurrent.TimeUnit;
import org.openqa.selenium.*;
import org.openqa.selenium.chrome.ChromeDriver;
import org.openqa.selenium.firefox.FirefoxDriver;

public  class MainTest
 {
    public static void main(String[] args)
    {

      WebDriver driver =null;
      System.setProperty("webdriver.chrome.driv
er", "F:\\selenium\\csharp\\chromedriver.exe");
      driver = new ChromeDriver();
      driver.manage().timeouts().pageLoadTimeou
t(20, TimeUnit.SECONDS);
      driver.manage().timeouts().implicitlyWait
(20, TimeUnit.SECONDS);

       try
        {
            driver.get("http://register.rediff.
com/register/register.php");
            driver.findElement(By.name("name"))
.sendKeys("ff89");

            driver.findElement(By.name("name"))
.sendKeys(Keys.TAB);
```

```
            Thread.sleep(3000);
            //driver.findElement(By.name("passwd"))
.click();
            driver.switchTo().alert().accept();
            Thread.sleep(4000);
             //driver.navigate();
             //driver.navigate("http://www.goog
le.com");
        }
          catch(Exception e)
          {
             System.out.println(e.toString());
          }

          finally
           {
              driver.close();
              driver.quit();
           }
        }
    }
```

16.3 Switching to frames

A webpage may contain multiple frames. To perform the operation on elements inside frame, we need to first switch to that frame and then we can use Webdriver methods on the web elements inside frame.

We can switch to frame using 3 different ways.

1. using index
2. using name
3. using any identification method like xpath, cssselector.

```
package seleniumtest;
```

```java
import org.openqa.selenium.By;
import org.openqa.selenium.WebDriver;
import org.openqa.selenium.WebElement;
import org.openqa.selenium.chrome.ChromeDriver;
import org.openqa.selenium.firefox.FirefoxDriver;

public  class MainTest
 {
   public static void main(String[] args)
    {
        WebDriver driver =null;
        System.setProperty("webdriver.chrome.dr
iver", "F:\\selenium\\csharp\\chromedriver.exe"
);
        driver = new ChromeDriver();

      try
      {
       driver.get("http://www.samplesite.com");

    //switch to the first frame in document
driver.switchTo().frame(0).findElement(By.id("d
d")).clear();

//switch to the frame having name =fname

driver.switchTo().frame("fname").findElement(By
.id("dd")).clear();

//switch to the frame having id = fid

WebElement e =driver.findElement(By.id("fid"));
driver.switchTo().frame(e).findElement(By.id("d
d")).clear();

        //driver.navigate();
        //driver.navigate("http://www.google.com"
);
    }
```

```
    catch(Exception e){}

    finally
    {
      driver.close();
      driver.quit();
    }

  }
}
```

16.4 Upload files in selenium web driver using AutoIT Script

Some times you will have to handle the file upload window using selenium web driver.
Selenium does not provide any such way to handle the window pop ups.

You can use AutoIT script to automate this task. AutoIT is a scripting language for Microsoft windows applications. You will have to download and install AutoIT from this url (https://www.autoitscript.com/site/autoit/downloads/)

Once downloaded, you can write below code in the script file and invoke that file code just when you need to handle the upload window. Semicolon(;) is used to mark the comments in AutoIT scripts.

```
;below line states Windows controller to wait
for the window with title Open to display.
```

Whatever is the name of window, you need to pass it here.

```
WinWaitActive("Open")

;below line will enter the file location to be
uploaded.
Send("C:\Users\sagar\Documents\onion_fennel_bis
que.jpg")

;finally we need to click on Ok or press enter
to start the upload process.
Send("{ENTER}")
```

Here is the complete example.

```java
package seleniumtest;

//autoIT
//TestNG
//Grid

//import the required classes
import java.text.SimpleDateFormat;
import java.util.Date;
import java.util.Set;
import java.util.concurrent.TimeUnit;
import org.openqa.selenium.By;
import org.openqa.selenium.WebDriver;
import org.openqa.selenium.*;
import org.openqa.selenium.chrome.ChromeDriver;

public  class AutoIT
 {
 public static void main(String[] args)
 {

     WebDriver driver =null;
     //set the driver path
```

```java
System.setProperty("webdriver.chrome.driver",
 "F:\\selenium\\csharp\\chromedriver.exe");

    System.setProperty("webdriver.ie.driver",
"F:\\selenium\\IEDriverServer_Win32_2.43.0\\IED
riverServer.exe");

    Date dNow = new Date( );


    //create new driver instance
    driver = new ChromeDriver();


driver.manage().timeouts().pageLoadTimeout(60,
TimeUnit.SECONDS);

driver.manage().timeouts().implicitlyWait(20,
TimeUnit.SECONDS);

    try
     {
      driver.get("https://www.pdftoword.com/");
      driver.findElement(By.id("file-
uploader")).click();
      //please note that below line calls the
AutoIT script which will handle the file upload
dialog in google chrome browser.Also note that
we need to provide the path of exe file which
is created after we compile and build the
AutoIT script.

Runtime.getRuntime().exec("F:\\selenium\\handle
file1.exe");

       //wait for 2 seconds
    Thread.sleep(5000);
    }
  catch(Exception e)
```

```
   {

   //print exception if any
   System.out.println(e.getMessage() );
   e.printStackTrace();
  }
   finally
   {

   //close the driver
   driver.close();
   //quit the driver.
   driver.quit();
  }
 }
}
```

16.5 Switching to default content

A browser window can have multiple frames inside it. A frame can have multiple child frames inside it.

Suppose there are 2 frames with names f1 and f2 at the top level. There is one child frame with name cf1 inside frame f1. To switch to frame cf1, you will have to use 2 lines of code.

//After below statement is executed, context is switched to frame - f1

```
driver.switchTo.frame("f1");
```

//Now we are inside frame f1. To switch the context to child frame - cf1, we will have to use below command.

```
driver.switchTo.frame("cf1");
```

Now we are inside frame cf1.

To switch the context to default content (main window content), you can use below line.

```
driver.switchTo().defaultContent();
```

Notice that while switching to the child frame - cf1, we have to switch the context to each parent frame. But to switch the context to main window, we can directly use defaultContent() method.

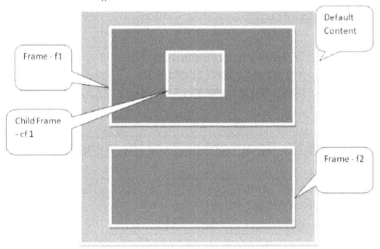

17. JavascriptExecutor

17.1 Executing custom Javascript

Below code will illustrate how we can execute java script in selenium webdriver.

Please note that we need to import below interface

```
import org.openqa.selenium.JavascriptExecutor;
```

Return innertext of the entire webpage using JavascriptExecutor

```
String x=((JavascriptExecutor)
driver).executeScript("return
document.documentElement.innerText;").toString(
);
```

Returning the document node of the webpage

```
WebElement p=(WebElement)((JavascriptExecutor)
driver).executeScript("return
document.documentElement;");
```

Finding the browser name using JavascriptExecutor

```java
public boolean getBrowserName()
{
        String agent = (String)
((JavascriptExecutor) driver)
.executeScript("return navigator.userAgent");
        if
(agent.toLowerCase().contains("chrome"))
        {
            return "Chrome";

        }else if
(agent.toLowerCase().contains("firefox"))
        {
            return "Firefox";

        }else if
(agent.toLowerCase().contains(".net"))
        {
            return "IE";

        }else if
(agent.toLowerCase().contains("macintosh") ||
agent.toLowerCase().contains("safari"))
        {
            return "Safari";

        }

}
```

Finding the screen width using JavascriptExecutor

```java
boolean isScreenWidthSmall()
  {
    Long width = (Long)(((JavascriptExecutor)
driver).executeScript
("return window.screen.width;"));

    if (width < 767)
        return true;
    else
        return false;
  }
```

Scrolling using JavascriptExecutor

```java
public void scrollToElement(WebElement element)
{
  ((JavascriptExecutor) driver).
executeScript("arguments[0].scrollIntoView();",
element);
    ((JavascriptExecutor)
driver).executeScript("window.scrollBy(0,-
111)");
}

public void scrollToTop()
{
  ((JavascriptExecutor)
driver).executeScript("window.scrollTo(200,200)
");

}
```

Get document state using JavascriptExecutor

```
public String getDocumentState()
{
  String state = ((JavascriptExecutor)driver).

 executeScript("return document.readyState;");
    return state;
}
```

Get Inner HTML of document using JavascriptExecutor

```
public String getInnerHtml(WebElement element)
{
  ((JavascriptExecutor)driver).
executeScript("return
arguments[0].innerHTML;",element);
}
```

Clicking on an element using JavascriptExecutor

```
protected void clickByJavaScript(WebElement
element)
{
 ((JavascriptExecutor)
driver).executeScript("arguments[0].click();",
element);
}
```

Complete example to execute javascript is given below in Java.

```java
package abc;
import java.util.concurrent.TimeUnit;
import org.openqa.selenium.By;
import org.openqa.selenium.WebDriver;
import org.openqa.selenium.WebElement;
import org.openqa.selenium.chrome.ChromeDriver;
import org.openqa.selenium.JavascriptExecutor;

public class ExecuteJavaScript
 {
 public static void main(String[] args)
 {
  System.setProperty("webdriver.chrome.driver",
  "F:\\chromedriver.exe");
  WebDriver driver =  new ChromeDriver();

  try
   {

   driver.manage().timeouts().setScriptTimeout(
20, TimeUnit.SECONDS);
   driver.manage().timeouts().pageLoadTimeout(5
0, TimeUnit.SECONDS);
   driver.manage().timeouts().implicitlyWait(20
, TimeUnit.SECONDS);

   driver.get("http://www.google.com");

String x =  ((JavascriptExecutor)
driver).executeScript("return
document.documentElement.innerText;").toString(
);

//sometimes we just want to click on the
elements so we can use below code
//below statement will click on webelement e.
```

```
//(JavascriptExecutor)
driver).executeScript("arguments[0].click();",e
);

//print the contents of the open page
System.out.println(x);

Thread.sleep(2000);
  }

  catch(Exception ex)
  {
    System.out.println(ex.toString());
  }
  finally
  {
    driver.close();
    driver.quit();
  }
 }
}
```

Javascript plays very important role when we are not able to perform complex operation on the element on the webpage. We can use all HTML DOM methods and properties when using javascript.

We can pass the parameters to the execute the script as shown below.

```
((JavascriptExecutor)
TestExecutor.wb).executeScript("arguments[0].cl
ick()",e);
```

In above code I have passed the webelement - e to executescript method. I can access the passed argument using arguments[] array.

17.2 How to scroll to element in Selenium

When automating the iOS applications running on iPad or iPhone in Safari, you encounter exceptions like element is not visible. But the same code works fine on other browsers like chrome and firefox.

So what is causing the issue in safari?

To fix this issue, you need to scroll to element and then work on that element.

Below method will accept the element and scroll to it.

```java
public void scrollToElement(WebElement element)
{

  ((JavascriptExecutor)
driver).executeScript("arguments[0].scrollIntoV
iew();",element)

  ((JavascriptExecutor)
driver).executeScript("window.scrollBy(0,-
100)")

}
```

17.3 Click not working Selenium

Sometimes click method of selenium does not work. In such situations, you can use below solutions.

1. Use javascript
2. Use Actions class

By using javascript, you can click on any element.

```
WebElement element =
driver.findElement(By.linkText("Log in"));
jsClick(element);

public static void jsClick(WebElement element)
{
  ((JavascriptExecutor) driver).executeScript
("arguments[0].click();",element);

}
```

By using Actions, you can click on any element.

```
WebElement element =
driver.findElement(By.linkText("Log in"));
clickByActions(element);

public static void clickByActions(WebElement
element)
{
 Actions builder = new Actions(driver);
 Action click = builder.click(element).build();
 click.perform();
}
```

17.4 Enter data in text box using JavaScript

Sometimes, sendKeys method does not work on text boxes. In such scenarios, you can use JavascriptExecutor to set the value in edit box. Below method takes 2 arguments. It sets the value passed in second argument in text box identified as first parameter.

```
protected void setValueByJavaScript(WebElement
element,String value)
{
        ((JavascriptExecutor)
driver).executeScript("arguments[0].value ='"+
value+"';", element);

}
```

17.5 Selecting drop down value using JavaScript

Sometimes you may encounter a scenario where selenium Select class can not be used to select the value from the drop down or list box in any browser like internet explorer, google chrome or firefox.
Sometime situation is more difficult because after selecting the value from drop down, other controls on the page get auto populated.
So basically there are 2 problems.
1. Selenium unable to select the value from the drop down.
2. Java script event does not get invoked. So other controls do not get auto populated.

We can solve above issues by below code.

```
WebElement c =
driver.findElement(By.xpath("//select[@name='em
pType']"));

((JavascriptExecutor)
driver).executeScript("arguments[0].value='X';"
,c);
```

Above script will select value X from the drop down.

After this you will have to trigger the on change event on the drop down using below code.

```
((JavascriptExecutor) driver).executeScript(
"var evt = document.createEvent('HTMLEvents');

evt.initEvent ('change', true, true);

arguments[0].dispatchEvent(evt);",c);
```

This will fire the drop down change event on the web list.

18. Frameworks with selenium

18.1 Keyword driven frameworks in Selenium

Keyword driven Automation Framework is very popular framework used in Selenium Webdriver with Java.
In this article I will explain you all details about how we can design and use keyword driven automation framework in Selenium Webdriver with Java along with example.

Keyword driven automation framework in Selenium Webdriver with Java - Introduction

In keyword driven automation framework we create the methods in Java that are mapped to the functionality of the application.

For example -
Suppose you have a bus ticket booking application which provides many features like

1. Login to the bus booking website
2. Search Buses with given source and destination and time
3. Select the bus tickets
4. Book bus tickets
5. Cancel bus tickets
6. View the booking history
7. Make the payment.

To automate the test cases for such web applications, We usually write the methods that perform specific task. For example we may write the searchBus method in Java which will search the buses for given source city, Destination city and Date.

Similarly we will create the methods for each functionality. The advantage of creating methods is that we can re-use these methods in multiple test cases with different input test data.

This speeds up the automation process with increased productivity.

The Components of keyword driven automation framework in Selenium Webdriver with Java

Each keyword driven automation framework has some common components as mentioned below.

1. Java Class Library with functionality specific methods.
2. Test Data Sheet (generally in excel format)
3. Selenium Webdriver with Java.
4. Reports in HTML format)
5. Main Java driver script

1. <u>Java Class Library with functionality specific methods.</u>

As explained earlier, we can create methods for each functionality in the application like bookTicket, makePayment etc.
Sample Java method is shown below to login to the web application.

```java
public static boolean Login()
{
  driver.navigate().to("http://www.abc.com");
  WebElement e1 =
driver.findElement(By.id("UserName"));
  e1.sendKeys("userid");
  WebElement e2 =
driver.findElement(By.id("Password"));
  e2.sendKeys("password");
WebElement e3 =
driver.findElement(By.name("submit"));
  e3.click();

  Boolean isPresent =
driver.findElements(By.className("logoutlink"))
.size()>0;

    if (isPresent == true)
     {
       //System.out.println("Login was
successful");
        return true;
     }
     else
     {
       //System.out.println("Login was not
successful");
        return false;
     }
```

```
}
//Please note that you can write the methods to
perform more complex operations in similar
//fashion
```

2. Test Data Sheet in Selenium Webdriver framework

As displayed in below figure, the data sheet contains below columns.

1. ID -Manual test case ID
2. Test_Case_Name - Name of the test case
3. Exec_Flag - Execution flag to tell if you want to execute this test case. Y means that test will be executed
4. Test_Step_Id - Step Id of the Test case
5. Test_Case_Steps - Step name of the test case
6. Keyword - The name of method in function library you want to call.
7. objectTypes - type of the web elements like webedit, weblist, webcheckbox etc
8. objectNames - Web element identification method and expression like xpath://td
9. objectValues - actual test data you want to enter in the webElement
10. parameter1 - extra parameter to drive the method control
11. parameter2 - one more parameter to drive the method control

ID	test_case_ name	Exec_ Flag	Test_st ep ID	Test_case_ steps	keyword	objectTypes	objectname s	objectvalues	param eter1	param eter2
1	insert order	Y	step1	login	login	winedit;win edit	Agent;;Pas	sagar;mercu ry;click		
2	fax order	N	step1	login	login	winedit;win edit	id;pwd	sagar;mercu ry		
			step2	Insertorde r	insertord er					
3	Delete order	N	step1	login	login	winedit;win edit	id;pwd	sagar;mercu ry		
			step2	Insertorde r	insertord er					

Sample test Datasheet in selenium webdriver in Java

3. Selenium Webdriver in Java

This is the driver instance you will create to execute the test cases.

Sample code to create a web driver instance is given below.

```
System.setProperty("webdriver.chrome.driver", "
F:\\selenium\\chromedriver.exe");
WebDriver driver =  new ChromeDriver();
```

4. Creating html Reports in Selenium Webdriver automation framework

You can create the html reports using file handling mechanism in Java.

Below code will delete the existing report file

```
if ((new File(c:\\reportfile.html)).exists() )
    (new File(c:\\reportfile.html)).delete();
```

171

Below code will append the data to the existing report file stored at given filePath

```java
public static void appendToFile(String
filePath,String data)
{
        //This function will be used to append
text data to filepath
        try
        {
          File temp = new File(filePath);
          FileWriter fw
= new FileWriter(temp,true);
          fw.append(data);
          fw.close();
        }
        catch(Exception e){}
}
```

Please note that you will need to import the classes in the package java.io to work with files.

5. Main driver script in Selenium webdriver automation framework

This is the main method and starting point for the framework code. The main responsibilities of this method are given below.

1. Read the test case steps from the datasheet one row at a time
2. Execute the method corresponding to the current step in the test case
3. Log the verification points in the html report file
4. Report the overall execution status like total failed/passed test cases, execution time

5. Send an email to all stakeholders regarding the execution status.

You will need to import the excel library provided by org.apache.poi

18.2 Reading and writing data in excel file

Here is the complete Java code to read and write from the excel sheet in Java. Please note that you will have to download and add POI library to current project from url (http://poi.apache.org/download.html)

The package org.apache.poi.hssf contains the xls implementations
The package org.apache.poi.xssf contains the xlsx implementations

```java
package framework;

import java.io.File;
import java.io.FileInputStream;
import java.io.FileOutputStream;
import java.util.Iterator;

import org.apache.poi.hssf.usermodel.HSSFSheet;
import
org.apache.poi.hssf.usermodel.HSSFWorkbook;
import org.apache.poi.ss.usermodel.Row;

public class Excel
 {
 /**
  * @param args
  */
 public static void main(String[] args)
 {
```

```java
FileInputStream file = null;
HSSFWorkbook workbook;

Futil.createHtmlHead(1);

  try
  {
     file = new FileInputStream(new
File("F:\\selenium\\batch.xls"));
     workbook = new HSSFWorkbook(file);
     HSSFSheet sheet = workbook.getSheetAt(0);
 Iterator<Row> rowIterator = sheet.iterator();
     int k=0;
     while (rowIterator.hasNext())
       {
         rowIterator.next();
         k++;
       }

 System.out.println("Total rows in the sheet " + k);
     int intRowCounter = 1;
     Row row =  sheet.getRow(intRowCounter);
 System.out.println("Data in the excel " +
readcell(row,2));

 row.getCell(1).setCellValue("salunke");
 FileOutputStream fos = new
FileOutputStream("F:\\selenium\\batch.xls");
    workbook.write(fos);
    fos.close();
  }
  catch(Exception ex)
  {
    System.out.println("Exception occured" +
ex.toString());
  }

  finally
  {
```

```java
   try
   {
      file.close();
   }
   catch(Exception ex)
   {
      System.out.println(ex.toString());
   }
}

 }//main method ends
//to read the data

 public static String readcell(Row rowObj,int
colNum)
  {
   String x="";
  try{
   if  (rowObj.getCell(colNum).getCellType() ==
1)
     x =
rowObj.getCell(colNum).getStringCellValue();
   else if
(rowObj.getCell(colNum).getCellType() == 0)
     x = "" +
(int)rowObj.getCell(colNum).getNumericCellValue
();
  }
  catch(Exception e)
  {
   x = "";
 //System.out.println(e.toString() + " while
reading a cell");
   }

   return x;
  }
```

```
 //to write the data
 public static void writeCell(Row rowObj,int
colNum, String data)
 {
    try
    {

rowObj.getCell(colNum).setCellValue((String)
data);

    }
  catch(Exception e)
    {
      System.out.println(e.toString() + " while
writing a cell");
    }
 }

} //class ends
```

18.3 Page object models

Major features of Page Object models are

1. It's a object oriented framework.
2. All application pages are modeled as Page classes. Each Page class has fields (Elements on the page). Each Page class has methods that get or set the values for the elements. This helps in the maintenance of the project as elements are not duplicated.
3. Step classes are created which can use multiple page models to perform specific operation like login, book a ticket, cancel a ticket, log out etc.
4. Test classes contain test methods which use Step classes to automate the test flow. From test class,

we pass on the input data to steps classes and steps classes pass that data to page classes.

Architectural diagram of Page Object models

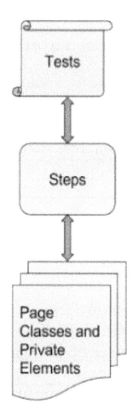

Example in Java - Page Object models

Steps to create page object models -
1. Identify all pages in the application and create a class for each page.
2. Identify elements and create methods to access to those elements.
3. Write the Step class to use one or multiple Page classes. This step class is optional as We can access

the Page members directly from Tests by instantiating the Page classes.

4. Then write the Test classes that uses steps to develop the test case.

For example - Consider this Selenium Test page (http://www.softpost.org/selenium-test-page/)

So sample page class for this page will look like below.

```java
package pages;

import org.openqa.selenium.By;
import org.openqa.selenium.WebDriver;
import pages.common.BasePage;

public class SeleniumTestPage extends BasePage
{
    private String
firstName="//td[contains(text(),'First Name')]"
+"//following-sibling::td//input";

  public SeleniumTestPage(WebDriver driver)
  {
    super(driver);
  driver.get("http://www.softpost.org/selenium-
test-page/");
  }

  public void setFirstName(String name)
  {
driver.findElement(By.xpath(firstName)).sendKey
s(name);
  }


  public String getFirstName()
  {
```

```
    return
driver.findElement(By.xpath(firstName)).getAttr
ibute("value");
    }
}
```

We can create instances of this class from our test and then perform any operation on that page.

```
package page_object_model_tests;

import org.junit.Assert;
import org.junit.Test;
import
page_object_model_tests.BaseTests.BaseTest;
import pages.SeleniumTestPage;

public class SamplePageTests extends BaseTest
{
    @Test     public void testPage()
    {
      SeleniumTestPage seleniumTestPage = new
SeleniumTestPage(driver);
      seleniumTestPage.setFirstName("Sagar");
      String name =
seleniumTestPage.getFirstName();
      Assert.assertTrue("Name
validation",name.equalsIgnoreCase("Sagar"));
    }
}
```

Above test will create the object of Page -
SeleniumTestPage and then use it's methods to interact with elements on the page.
Below code shows the BaseTest class. All tests inherit from this class.

```
package page_object_model_tests.BaseTests;

import org.junit.AfterClass;
import org.junit.BeforeClass;
import org.openqa.selenium.WebDriver;
import
org.openqa.selenium.firefox.FirefoxDriver;
import java.util.concurrent.TimeUnit;

public class BaseTest
{
    protected static WebDriver driver ;
    @BeforeClass    public static void init()
    {
        driver = new FirefoxDriver();

driver.manage().timeouts().implicitlyWait(20,
TimeUnit.SECONDS);
        driver.manage().window().maximize();
    }
    @AfterClass     public static void clean()
     {
        driver.close();
        driver.quit();
     }
}
```

Below code shows the BasePage class. All pages inherit from this base page class.

```
import org.openqa.selenium.WebDriver;

/** * Created by Sagar on 26-03-2016. */
public class BasePage
    {
      protected WebDriver driver;

      public BasePage(WebDriver driver)
      {
          this.driver = driver;
      }

      //Common methods will be put here
}
```

18.4 Page Factory Model

Key features of Page Factory model

1. Object oriented
2. Most of the features are similar to Page Object Models
3. One primary difference between page object model and page factory model is that web elements are initialized in different manner.

Here is the sample Page class for a page (http://www.softpost.org/selenium-test-page/)

```
package pages;
```

```java
import org.openqa.selenium.By;
import org.openqa.selenium.WebDriver;
import org.openqa.selenium.WebElement;
import org.openqa.selenium.support.FindBy;
import org.openqa.selenium.support.PageFactory;
import pages.common.BasePage;

public class SeleniumTestPageUsingFactory
extends BasePage
{
    public
SeleniumTestPageUsingFactory(WebDriver driver)
    {
        super(driver);
        PageFactory.initElements(driver,this);
    }

    @FindBy(id = "fn" )
    WebElement firstName;

    public void setFirstName(String name)
    {
        firstName.sendKeys(name);
    }

    public String getFirstName()
    {
        return firstName.getAttribute("value");
    }
}
```

Note how we have used PageFactory.initElements method to initialize the elements on the page.

We can instantiate this page class and perform operations on Page elements. Below class demonstrates how we can use this Page class in tests.

```
package page_object_model_tests;

import org.junit.Assert;
import org.junit.Test;
import
page_object_model_tests.BaseTests.BaseTest;
import pages.SeleniumTestPage;
import pages.SeleniumTestPageUsingFactory;

public class SamplePageTestsUsingFactory
extends BaseTest
{

    @Test      public void testPage()
    {
      SeleniumTestPageUsingFactory
seleniumTestPage;
      seleniumTestPage  = new
SeleniumTestPageUsingFactory(driver);
      seleniumTestPage.setFirstName("Sagar");
      String name =
seleniumTestPage.getFirstName();
      Assert.assertTrue("Name
validation",name.equalsIgnoreCase("Sagar"));
    }
}
```

18.5 Writing JUnit tests

JUnit framework is a popular unit testing framework in Testing world.

In this Book, you will get to know how to write junit tests with selenium webdriver. All you need to write the JUnit tests is JUnit provider. Just add that dependency in your Java project and start writing the tests.

How to add JUnit dependency in your project?

Most of the maven and Gradle projects POM and build.gradle file is created with JUnit dependency automatically when you create such projects. But in case your POM.xml file does not have JUnit dependency, just add below lines in dependencies section your POM.xml

```
<dependency>
    <groupId>junit</groupId>
    <artifactId>junit</artifactId>
    <version>4.11</version>
    <scope>test</scope>
</dependency>
```

If you are using Gradle based project, just add below line in build.gradle file.

testCompile group: 'junit', name: 'junit', version: '4.11'

How to write JUnit tests for Selenium Webdriver?

We need to create a Class and methods in it annotated with @Test as shown in below example. You can execute this test by pressing CTRL+SHIFT+F10 in Intellij IDEA or you can just right click on the method and click on Run using JUnit.

```
public class FirefoxTests
{

    static WebDriver driver;

```

```
   @Test      public void launchChrome() throws
Exception
    {
        driver = new FirefoxDriver();

driver.manage().timeouts().implicitlyWait(10,
TimeUnit.SECONDS);
        driver.manage().window().maximize();

driver.get("http://www.softpost.org/selenium-
test-page/");
        driver.close();
        driver.quit();
    }
}
```

Executing Selenium JUnit tests with Maven

You can also run JUnit tests using Maven Goals. Maven
uses Surefire plug-in to run the tests during Test phase.
You can also configure the Surefire plug-in to include or
exclude the specific tests.

Just type below command in command prompt and all
your tests will get executed.

mvn test

If you want to run specific tests, you can pass -Dtest
parameter which runs tests in specific class. Say you want
to run tests in only BookingTests class, then use below
command.

```
mvn test -Dtest=BookingTests
```

Executing Selenium JUnit tests with Gradle

You can also run JUnit tests using Gradle tasks.
Just type below command in command prompt and all
your tests will get executed.

gradle test

18.6 How to use TestNG

TestNG is the next generation testing framework. You can
easily integrate your selenium scripts in TestNG.

Please follow below steps to run TestNG tests in Eclipse.

1. Download TestNG
   at http://testng.org/doc/download.html
2. Then Create a TestNG class in any project.
3. Define test methods in that class using @Test
   annotation
4. Right click on the TestNG class and run as TestNG
   class.

In below example, we have created a TestNG class called
NewTest with 2 test methods Test1 and Test2.

```
package framework;

import org.testng.Assert;
```

```java
import org.testng.annotations.AfterSuite;
import org.testng.annotations.AfterTest;
import org.testng.annotations.BeforeSuite;
import org.testng.annotations.BeforeTest;
import org.testng.annotations.Test;

public class NewTest
 {
  @Test
  public void Test1()
  {
     //Test something here.
     Assert.assertNotNull("abc");
  }

  @Test
  public void Test2()
  {
     //Test something here.

     Assert.assertNull("jj");
  }

  @BeforeSuite
  public void beforeSuite()
  {
      //this method is called once before test
execution starts

//here you can write a code to launch the
selenium web driver.
  }

  @AfterSuite
  public void afterSuite()
  {
      //this method is called once after test
execution ends.
```

```
//here you can write a code to close and quit
the selenium web driver.
   }
}
```

18.7 Data driven frameworks

One of them is Data driven framework. This kind of framework is used when we need to test same application flows using different combinations of data. Different types of applications need different types of frameworks. We must use Data driven framework in a situation where there are limited number of Application flows but there is wide variety of data that is consumed by application.

For example - Consider a simple register functionality of a website. You need to verify that password should meet below criteria.

1. At least 8 characters in length
2. Should contain alphanumeric characters
3. Should contain at least one non-alphanumeric character.
4. Should contains at least one lower case and one upper case letter.

All we need to do to test this functionality is write simple test which will enter values in the password textbox and verify if the password test passes. In this scenario, all steps are same except test data. That is when we should Data driven frameworks. We can store data in either excel sheet or database.
Test reads each set of data and repeats same steps.

The main difference between keyword driven and data driven frameworks is that in keyword driven frameworks we have multiple application flows and operations. Generally, in most of the projects hybrid frameworks are used as application has multiple flows and various combinations of data at the same time.

18.8 Framework Utilities

Let us take a look at below utility methods.

18.8.1 Killing processes with name

We can kill processes in Java using below code. In below example, all processes with names firefox, ieexplore and chrome will be killed in Linux or windows.

```
public static void killProcesses()
{
   try
   {
     String [] processNames =
{"firefox","iexplore","chrome"};
       for (String process : processNames)
       {
          if (SystemUtils.IS_OS_LINUX)
          {
             String[] command = {"/bin/sh",
 "-c", "ps -ef | grep -w "+
 process +" | grep -v grep | awk '/[0-9]/{print
$2}' | xargs kill -9 "};

StringBuffer output = new StringBuffer();
   try
   {
   Process p = Runtime.getRuntime().exec(cmd);
   List<String> result =
IOUtils.readLines(p.getInputStream());
```

```
    for (String line : result)
    {
      System.out.println(line);
      output.append(line);
    }
  }
  catch (Exception e)
  {
    e.printStackTrace();
  }


 }
 else if (SystemUtils.IS_OS_WINDOWS)
 {

Runtime.getRuntime().exec("taskkill /F /IM "+
process +".exe");
 }
              }
}
 catch (IOException e)
 {
    e.printStackTrace();
 }
}
```

18.8.2 Generating unique random numbers

Below code generates unique random numbers and
alphanumeric values in Java.

```
Calendar date = Calendar.getInstance();
```

```java
        String day =
String.valueOf(date.get(Calendar.DAY_OF_MONTH));

        String month =
String.valueOf(date.get(Calendar.MONTH)+1);

        tring year =
String.valueOf(date.get(Calendar.YEAR));

            if (day.length()==1){day = "0"+day;}
            if (month.length()==1){month =
"0"+month;}

        String time =
String.valueOf(date.get(Calendar.HOUR_OF_DAY))
+ String.valueOf(date.get(Calendar.MINUTE)) +
 String.valueOf(date.get(Calendar.SECOND));

        System.out.println("Unique timeStamp is
-> " + time +
 year + month + day);

        //Generates random hash string
containing numbers and digits
        UUID id1 = UUID.randomUUID();

        System.out.println("Unique id is -> "+
id1);

        java.util.Date date1= new
java.util.Date();

        System.out.println("Unique timestamp is
-> " +
 new Timestamp(date1.getTime()));
```

18.8.3 Get formatted amount

Below method returns the amount in double format in Java.

```java
double getFormattedAmount(String amount)
{

String digitalAmount =
amount.replaceAll("[\$,]","");

return Double.parseDouble(digitalAmount);

}
```

18.8.4 Date and time utilities

Adding or subtracting the specific duration from the date

```java
static Calendar calculateDate(String date)
{
    int durationToBeAddedOrSubtracted;
    Calendar newDate = Calendar.getInstance();
    //-20 years
        durationToBeAddedOrSubtracted =
Integer.parseInt(date.split(" ")[0]);

    if (date.toLowerCase().contains("months"))
    {
       newDate.add(Calendar.MONTH,
durationToBeAddedOrSubtracted);
    }
 else if (date.toLowerCase().contains("years"))
 {
   newDate.add(Calendar.YEAR,
durationToBeAddedOrSubtracted);
 }
 else
```

```
{
   newDate.add(Calendar.DATE,
durationToBeAddedOrSubtracted);
 }
   return newDate;
}
```

Getting the parts from a date in Java.

```java
public void getDateParts(Calendar date)
{
  String day =
String.valueOf(date.get(Calendar.DAY_OF_MONTH));
   String month =
String.valueOf(date.get(Calendar.MONTH)+1);
  String year =
String.valueOf(date.get(Calendar.YEAR));

   if (day.length()==1)
   {
     day = "0"+day;
   }
   if (month.length()==1)
   {
     month = "0"+month;
   }

}
```

Creating Calendar object from the date parts in Java.

```java
int day = Integer.parseInt(dob[0]);
 int month = Integer.parseInt(dob[1])-1;
 int year = Integer.parseInt(dob[2]);
```

```
Calendar newDate = Calendar.getInstance();
newDate.set(year, month, day, 0, 0);
```

18.8.5 Executing Linux and windows commands

Below example illustrates how to execute the Windows and Linux commands in Java.Note that we are using **org.apache.commons.lang.SystemUtils** class to determine OS type.

```
if(SystemUtils.IS_OS_LINUX)
  {
    cmd= [ "/bin/bash", "-c", " ps -
fu`whoami`|grep p1|grep -v grep" ]
  }
  else if (SystemUtils.IS_OS_WINDOWS)
  {
    cmd= ["bash", "-c", "tasklist | grep p1"]
  }

  StringBuffer output = new StringBuffer();
  try
  {
    Process p = Runtime.getRuntime().exec(cmd);
    List<String> result =
IOUtils.readLines(p.getInputStream());
      for (String line : result)
        {
          System.out.println(line);
          output.append(line);
        }
    }
  catch (Exception e)
  {
    e.printStackTrace();
  }
  return output.toString();
```

18.8.6 Setting and getting System Properties

To set the System property

```
System.setProperty("p1","v1");
```

Loading System properties from a settings file say xyz.properties

```
Properties prop = new Properties();

try
{
  InputStream inputStream =
URLReader.class.getClassLoader().
  getResourceAsStream("xyz.properties");
  prop.load(inputStream);
}
catch (IOException ex)
{

}
```

Reading System property

```
System.getProperty("os.name")
System.getProperty("user.dir");
```

Similarly we can read user.timezone, user.home, java.version, file.separator

Reading all System properties

```
System.getProperties().list(System.out);
```

18.8.7 Extract digits from a String

Many times, we have to verify the numbers from a given string.

Below Java code will help get the digits from the string.

```
public String extractDigits(String str)
{
    return str.replaceAll("[^0-9]","");
}
```

18.9 Taking a screenshot of webpage

We can take a screenshot easily using below code. Please note that we need to import below classes/interfaces.

```
import org.apache.commons.io.FileUtils;
import org.openqa.selenium.TakesScreenshot;
import org.openqa.selenium.OutputType;
```

Full example in Java to take a screenshot is given below.

```java
package temp;
import java.io.File;
import java.util.concurrent.TimeUnit;
import org.apache.commons.io.FileUtils;
import org.openqa.selenium.OutputType;
import org.openqa.selenium.TakesScreenshot;
import org.openqa.selenium.WebDriver;
import org.openqa.selenium.chrome.ChromeDriver;
import org.openqa.selenium.firefox.FirefoxDriver;

//import com.sun.jna.platform.FileUtils;
@SuppressWarnings("unused")
public class OpenGoogle
{
    public static void main(String [] arg)
    {
System.setProperty("webdriver.chrome.driver", "
C:\\Selenuim\\chromedriver2.8.exe");
WebDriver driver =  new ChromeDriver();


try
{
driver.manage().timeouts().implicitlyWait(20,
TimeUnit.SECONDS);
driver.manage().timeouts().pageLoadTimeout(50,T
imeUnit.SECONDS);
//driver.navigate().to("http://www.google.com");


driver.get("http://www.google.com/");


//take a screenshot
```

```
File scrFile =
((TakesScreenshot)driver).getScreenshotAs(Outpu
tType.FILE);


//save the screenshot in png format on the
disk.
FileUtils.copyFile(scrFile, new File("c:\\sagar
\\screenshot.png"));


}


catch(Exception e)
{
   System.out.println("Exception - > " +
e.toString());
}
finally
{
   driver.close();
   driver.quit();
}
}        //main function ends

}//class ends
```

When any test case fails, we usually take Screenshot at runtime to help us in analysing the executed test cases to find the state of web application when failure occured.

18.10 Logging framework in Selenium

log4j is very popular logging framework in Java.
You can specify the settings of the framework using either XML file or properties file.
Key things to know about log4j framework are –

1. It can be used to send the log messages to multiple appenders like file, console etc
2. Various log level are OFF, FATAL, ERROR, WARN, INFO, DEBUG and TRACE.
3. If you set the Log level as WARN, then only higher level (FATAL and ERROR)log messages are logged.
4. It allows you to set the log level at root level as well as class level.
5. We can restrict the log level for each appender using threshold parameter.

Here is the sample log4j.properties file. We usually keep this file in resources directory of the Java project.

```
#We have specified the logging level as INFO
and 2 appenders are set up

log4j.rootLogger=INFO, mystdoutappender,
myfileappender

# Send log messages to file with name
mylog4j.log

log4j.appender.myfileappender=org.apache.log4j.
FileAppender

log4j.appender.myfileappender.File=mylog4j.log

log4j.appender.myfileappender.layout=org.apache
.log4j.PatternLayout

log4j.appender.myfileappender.layout.Conversion
Pattern=%d{yyyy-MM-dd HH:mm:ss} %-5p %c{1}:%L -
%m%n
```

```
# Send log messages to console - Standard
Output Stream

log4j.appender.mystdoutappender=org.apache.log4
j.ConsoleAppender

log4j.appender.mystdoutappender.Target=System.o
ut

log4j.appender.mystdoutappender.layout=org.apac
he.log4j.PatternLayout

log4j.appender.mystdoutappender.layout.Conversi
onPattern=%d{yyyy-MM-dd HH:mm:ss} %-5p %c{1}:%L
- %m%n
```

Here is the sample class using logger.

```java
import org.apache.log4j.Logger;

import org.junit.Test;
/**
 * Created by Sagar on 04-07-2016.
 */
public class LogTest
 {
   final static Logger logger =
Logger.getLogger(LogTest.class);

    @Test
    public void test1()
    {
      //OFF, FATAL, ERROR, WARN, INFO, DEBUG and TRACE
      logger.fatal("Fatal message");
      logger.error("Dump error");
       logger.warn("Warning baby");
       logger.info("Hello - This is info");
        //Below messages will not be logged as
we have set the log level as INFO
```

```
        logger.debug("Debug message");
        logger.trace("Trace message");
    }

}
```

Here is the output of above code.

2016-07-14 19:09:43 FATAL LogTest:13 - Fatal message
2016-07-14 19:09:43 ERROR LogTest:14 - Dump error
2016-07-14 19:09:43 WARN LogTest:15 - Warning baby
2016-07-14 19:09:43 INFO LogTest:16 - Hello - This is info
Process finished with exit code 0

19. BDD frameworks

19.1 Cucumber

Cucumber is one of the most popular BDD testing frameworks. In this article, you will learn how to write the feature files and step definitions for running Selenium tests.

What tools you will need to run cucumber tests?

1. JAVA IDE - Intellij IDEA
2. JDK
3. Maven or Gradle
4. Cucumber API
5. Cucumber plug-in for Intellij IDEA
6. Intellij IDEA plug-ins for **Gherkin and Cucumber for Java**

You will need to add below dependencies in your project to use Cucumber API

```
testCompile 'info.cukes:cucumber-java:1.2.4'testCompile 'info.cukes:cucumber-junit:1.2.4'
```

How to write tests using Cucumber?

Below example shows how you can write a simple cucumber test class. When we run that Test class, all features in the src/test/resources directory are run. If there are no step definitions written for the steps in feature file, it creates sample step methods for you.

```
package cucumber_tests;

import cucumber.api.CucumberOptions;
import cucumber.api.junit.Cucumber;
import org.junit.runner.RunWith;

/** * Created by Sagar on 27-03-2016. */
@RunWith(Cucumber.class)
@CucumberOptions(features =
"src/test/resources/")
public class CucumberTests
{
}
```

I had a feature file as shown below. But I did not write any steps.

```
Feature:Simple Selenium test
  Scenario: To check page loading
    Given I am on "http://www.softpost.org"
home page
    When I click on "Selenium Test page" link
    Then I land on Selenium Test Page
```

so after running above class, in the console I noticed that sample step methods are created.

```
1 Scenarios (1 undefined)
3 Steps (3 undefined)
0m0.000s
```

You can implement missing steps with the snippets below:

```java
@Given("^I am on \"([^\"]*)\" home page$")
public void i_am_on_home_page(String arg1)
throws Throwable
{
    // Write code here that turns the phrase
above into concrete actions
    throw new PendingException();
}

@When("^I click on \"([^\"]*)\" link$")
public void i_click_on_link(String arg1) throws
Throwable
{
    // Write code here that turns the phrase
above into concrete actions
    throw new PendingException();
}

@Then("^I land on Selenium Test Page$")
public void i_land_on_Selenium_Test_Page()
throws Throwable
{
    // Write code here that turns the phrase
above into concrete actions
    throw new PendingException();
}
```

Process finished with exit code 0.

After that I just copied all these methods and pasted into the steps class . Then I updated all test methods.

```java
package steps;

import cucumber.api.PendingException;
import cucumber.api.java.After;
import cucumber.api.java.Before;
import cucumber.api.java.en.Given;
import cucumber.api.java.en.Then;
import cucumber.api.java.en.When;
import cucumber.runtime.junit.FeatureRunner;
import org.openqa.selenium.By;
import org.openqa.selenium.WebDriver;
import org.openqa.selenium.firefox.FirefoxDriver;

import java.util.concurrent.TimeUnit;

/** * Created by Sagar on 27-03-2016. */
public class step_definitions
{
    WebDriver driver;
    @Before
  public void init()
  {
    driver = new FirefoxDriver();
  driver.manage().timeouts().implicitlyWait(20,
TimeUnit.SECONDS);
    driver.manage().window().maximize();
  }

    @Given("^I am on \"([^\"]*)\" home page$")
    public void i_am_on_home_page(String arg1)
throws Throwable
    {
        driver.get("http://www.softpost.org");
    }

    @When("^I click on \"([^\"]*)\" link$")
```

```
    public void i_click_on_link(String arg1)
throws Throwable
    {
      driver.findElement(By.LinkText("Selenium
Test Page")).click();
    }

    @Then("^I land on Selenium Test Page$")
    public void i_land_on_Selenium_Test_Page()
throws Throwable
    {
      assert
driver.findElements(By.id("fn")).size() > 0;
    }

    @After
    public void clean()
    {
        driver.close();
        driver.quit();
    }
}
```

After that I ran the test class but still Cucumber was unable to find the step definitions. Then I updated cucumber options as described below.

```
@RunWith(Cucumber.class)
@CucumberOptions(
        features = "src/test/resources",
        glue = {"steps"}
)
```

Notice that how I have added glue in the cucumber options. This is important to note that glue should be configured to be the package name in which your step definitions exist. While features option can have the value as directory name.

Another thing to note is that we can use lambda expressions to write step definitions. But for that you will have to use Java 8.
You may encounter below error when working with lambda expressions.
invalid method declaration return type required cucumber
To fix this error, you need to use below syntax.

```
public class lambda_steps implements En
{
    public lambda_steps()
    {
        Given("^I am on softpost\\.org home
page$", () -> {

        });
    }
}
```

20. Miscellaneous

20.1 Viewing the remote machine desktop of Linux using VNC

Most of the times, tests are run on the remote Linux machines. We can view the execution on remote Linux machine using virtual desktop. We need below 2 binaries running on the server.

1. xvfb - Virtual frame buffer - display server that implements X11 display server protocol. It does not show anything on screen. Another option is Xdummy. So in short, xvfb creates the virtual display in memory.
2. VNC Server - xvnc - Virtual network computing (Virtual display server). RealVNC, x11vnc and TightVNC are other tools that you can use. In short, VNC server allows you to start the server attached to
display created by xvfb.
3. On the client side, you need to install VNC client. VNC client connects to the VNC server allowing you to view the virtual display.

Starting the virtual display and VNC server

```
if [ -z "${DISPLAY}" ]
then
    echo "DISPLAY environment variable is not set"
    exit 1
fi

XVFB_RUNNING=`ps -efa | grep "Xvfb :97" | grep -v grep | cat`
```

```
if [ ! -z "${XVFB_RUNNING}" ]
then
    echo Xvfb is running: ${XVFB_RUNNING}
    exit 2
fi
XVNC_RUNNING=`ps -efa | grep "Xvnc" | grep -v
grep | cat`
if [ ! -z "${XVNC_RUNNING}" ]
then
    echo Xvnc is running: ${XVNC_RUNNING}
    exit 2
fi


rm -rf /tmp/.X*
/usr/bin/Xvfb :97 -screen 0 1280x1024x24
1>/dev/null 2>&1 &
/usr/bin/vncserver "$DISPLAY" -geometry
1280x1024
```

Killing all processes with name Xvnc

```
/usr/bin/killall -q -u `whoami` Xvnc | cat
```

XVFB also allows you to run the Firefox tests on Linux in headless manner. RealVNC also provides VNC server and clients.

Then from the VNC client we can connect to the VNC server at port say 97 and view the virtual display.

20.2 Selenium IDE Add-On for Firefox

Selenium IDE is a Firefox Add-On that can be used to record and playback the Selenium scripts. We can also export the scripts to various programming languages like C#, Java, Ruby and Python.

You can download the Add-On XPI file from the link - https://addons.mozilla.org/en-US/firefox/addon/selenium-ide/

Next you can install the Add-On in Firefox. Once installation is successful you will notice the Selenium IDE menu in Tools as shown in below image.

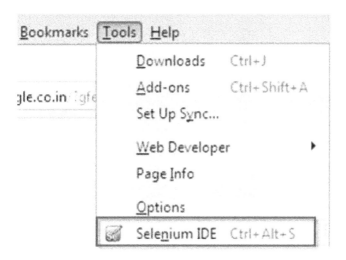

Selenium IDE menu

Below image shows the Selenium IDE GUI. We can record the script by clicking on red circle icon.

Below image shows that we can export the recorded script to Ruby, Python, Java, C# etc.

20.3 EventListeners

When Selenium performs any of the operations like click, navigate etc, events are fired.
We can write custom code when these events are fired.

We will need to create a class that implements the methods to be called after event is fired.

Below class implements the WebDriverEventListener.

```
package chrometest;

import org.openqa.selenium.By;
import org.openqa.selenium.WebDriver;
import org.openqa.selenium.WebElement;
import
org.openqa.selenium.support.events.WebDriverEve
ntListener;

/**
 * Created by Sagar on 22-06-2016.
 */
public class ListenerImplementation   implements
WebDriverEventListener
{
    @Override
    public void beforeNavigateTo(String s,
WebDriver webDriver)
    {
        System.out.println("Before navigating
to " + s);
    }

    @Override
    public void afterNavigateTo(String s,
WebDriver webDriver)
    {

    }

    @Override
    public void beforeNavigateBack(WebDriver
webDriver)
    {

    }

    @Override
```

```java
    public void afterNavigateBack(WebDriver
webDriver)
    {

    }

    @Override
    public void beforeNavigateForward(WebDriver
webDriver)
    {

    }

    @Override
    public void afterNavigateForward(WebDriver
webDriver)
    {

    }

    @Override
    public void beforeFindBy(By by, WebElement
webElement, WebDriver webDriver)
    {
        System.out.println("Before find by");
    }

    @Override
    public void afterFindBy(By by, WebElement
webElement, WebDriver webDriver)
    {

    }

    @Override
    public void beforeClickOn(WebElement
webElement, WebDriver webDriver)
    {

    }
```

```java
    @Override
    public void afterClickOn(WebElement
webElement, WebDriver webDriver)
    {

    }

    @Override
    public void beforeChangeValueOf(WebElement
webElement, WebDriver webDriver)
    {

    }

    @Override
    public void afterChangeValueOf(WebElement
webElement, WebDriver webDriver)
    {

    }

    @Override
    public void beforeScript(String s,
WebDriver webDriver)
    {

    }

    @Override
    public void afterScript(String s, WebDriver
webDriver)
    {

    }

    @Override
    public void onException(Throwable
throwable, WebDriver webDriver)
    {
```

```
            System.out.println("Exception");
        }
}
```

Next we need to register the instance of this class with driver as shown in highlighted code
below. beforeNavigateTo method is called when execute below code. In fact, all the methods for corresponding events are called automatically.

```
package chrometest;
import org.junit.Test;
import org.openqa.selenium.WebDriver;
import org.openqa.selenium.chrome.ChromeDriver;
import
org.openqa.selenium.support.events.EventFiringWebDriver;
import java.util.concurrent.TimeUnit;
/** * Created by Sagar on 17-02-2016. */
public class LaunchEventFiringChrome
  {
      static WebDriver driver = null;

      @Test
    public void launchChromeTest() throws Exception
      {
    System.setProperty("webdriver.chrome.driver",
    "C:\\Users\\Sagar\\Videos\\chromedriver_win32\\chromedriver.exe");

      driver = new ChromeDriver();

EventFiringWebDriver eventFiringWebDriverDriver =
  new EventFiringWebDriver(driver);
```

```
  ListenerImplementation listenerImplementation
=
new ListenerImplementation();

eventFiringWebDriverDriver.register(listenerImp
lementation);

eventFiringWebDriverDriver.manage().timeouts().
implicitlyWait
(10, TimeUnit.SECONDS);

eventFiringWebDriverDriver.manage().window().ma
ximize();

 String domain = "http://www.softpost.org";
 eventFiringWebDriverDriver.get(domain);

System.out.println(eventFiringWebDriverDriver.g
etTitle());
 eventFiringWebDriverDriver.close();
 eventFiringWebDriverDriver.quit();


    }
}
```

21. Integration with CI servers

21.1 Integration with TeamCity

In this topic, you will learn how to set up a build steps for maven project in TeamCity.

As shown in below image, you have to select runner type as Maven. Then you have to provide the goals to be executed. By default, it uses POM.xml in the root directory of the project. You may also run code coverage process along with test goal which gives report on how many classes were covered by tests.

Here is the list of some of the popular maven goals that can be used.

1. test - execute tests using surefire plugin. We can also pass various parameters to maven JUnit test goal and maven testNG test goal
2. verify - executes unit tests as well as does verification provided by plugins
3. install
4. site
5. deploy

maven build step in TeamCity

Below image shows that sample build log.

maven build log in TeamCity

21.2 Running Selenium tests using Jenkins and GIT

We can run selenium tests using Jenkins very easily.

How to set up Jenkins?

1. Download Jenkins.
2. Install git client
3. Set up maven task

Configuring Jenkins and running selenium tests

Jenkins server can be accessed @ localhost:8080
Please have a look at below images of Jenkins server.

1. Go to localhost:8080 to open Jenkins Home screen
2. Then configure JDK and Maven
3. Then install git plug-in
4. Then create new maven job
5. In maven job configuration, specify the git details (git url where your selenium tests are kept) and build trigger.
6. Then Specify Maven goal
7. Once Job is saved, you can manually run it or wait until it gets triggered automatically.
8. When the job is running, you can view the console output as well.

Jenkins Server Home Screen

JDK

JDK installations

JDK
Name   JDK1 7

JAVA_HOME   C \Program Files\Java\jdk1 7 0_79

Install automatically

Jenkins Server - Maven Configuration

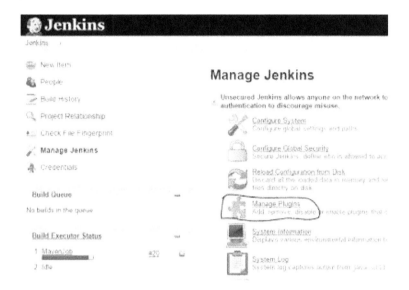

Jenkins Server - Manage Plug-ins

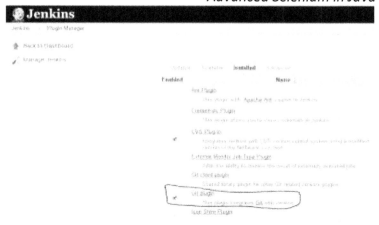

Jenkins Server - Install Git Plug-ins

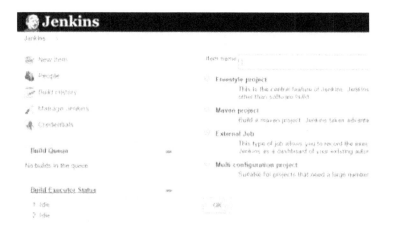

Jenkins Server - Create new Maven Project

Source Code Management

○ None
○ CVS
○ CVS Projectset
* Git
Repositories

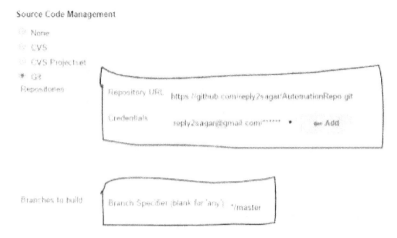

Repository URL   https://github.com/reply2sagar/AutomationRepo.git

Credentials   reply2sagar@gmail.com/******* ●   Add

Branches to build

Branch Specifier (blank for 'any')   */master

Jenkins Server - GIT configuration

Subversion

Build Triggers

☑ Build whenever a SNAPSHOT dependency is built

☐ Build after other projects are built

☑ Build periodically

Schedule

H/55 * * * *

Would last have run at Sunday, 27 March.

☐ Poll SCM

Pre Steps

Add pre-build step ▾

Build

Root POM

pom.xml

Goals and options

test

Jenkins Server - Build trigger and goal

S	W	Name ↓	Last Success	Last Failure	Last Duration	
All	+					
⬤		MavenJob	13 min - #20	1 day 11 hr - #10	3 min 14 sec	⊘

Jenkins Server - Running build

Console Output

```
Started by user anonymous
Building in workspace C:\Program Files (x86)\Jenkins\jobs\MavenJob\workspace
 > git.exe rev-parse --is-inside-work-tree # timeout=10
Fetching changes from the remote Git repository
 > git.exe config remote.origin.url https://github.com/reply2sagar/AutomationRepo.git # timeout=10
Fetching upstream changes from https://github.com/reply2sagar/AutomationRepo.git
 > git.exe --version # timeout=10
using .gitcredentials to set credentials
 > git.exe config --local credential.username reply2sagar@gmail.com # timeout=10
 > git.exe config --local credential.helper store --file=\"C:\\WINDOWS\TEMP\git1406474874122602615.credentials\" # timeout=10
 > git.exe -c core.askpass=true fetch --tags --progress https://github.com/reply2sagar/AutomationRepo.git
+refs/heads/*:refs/remotes/origin/*
 > git.exe config --local --remove-section credential # timeout=10
 > git.exe rev-parse "refs/remotes/origin/master^{commit}" # timeout=10
 > git.exe rev-parse "refs/remotes/origin/origin/master^{commit}" # timeout=10
Checking out Revision b1359e14a337f0f140c8c60cd7c6cd316445ae66 (refs/remotes/origin/master)
 > git.exe config core.sparsecheckout # timeout=10
 > git.exe checkout -f b1359e14a337f0f140c8c60cd7c6cd316445ae66
 > git.exe rev-list b1359e14a337f0f140c8c60cd7c6cd316445ae66 # timeout=10
Parsing POMs
[workspace] $ "C:\Program Files\Java\jdk1.7.0_79/bin/java" -cp "C:\Program Files (x86)\Jenkins\plugins\maven-plugin\WEB-
INF\lib\maven31-agent-1.5.jar;C:\maven\apache-maven-3.3.9\boot\plexus-classworlds-2.5.2.jar;C:\maven\apache-maven-3.3.9/conf
jenkins.maven3.agent.Maven31Main C:\maven\apache-maven-3.3.9 "C:\Program Files (x86)\Jenkins\war\WEB-INF\lib\remoting-2.52.3
"C:\Program Files (x86)\Jenkins\plugins\maven-plugin\WEB-INF\lib\maven31-interceptor-1.5.jar" "C:\Program Files
(x86)\Jenkins\plugins\maven-plugin\WEB-INF\lib\maven3-interceptor-commons-1.5.jar" 50213
```

Jenkins Server - Console output

21.3 Bamboo

In your Selenium project, add few selenium tests as mentioned below.
A typical Selenium test project includes few test classes. Each test class extends the base class where in we define before test and after test methods. In before test method, we create the webdriver instance and also perform test initialization tasks. In after test method, we close the driver and also perform clean up tasks like closing processes created during test run.

Below is the sample base class for all Selenium Test classes.

```java
package seleniumtests;
import org.junit.Before;
import org.junit.After;
import org.openqa.selenium.WebDriver;
import
org.openqa.selenium.firefox.FirefoxDriver;

public class BaseTest
  {
      public WebDriver driver;
      @Before
      public void init()
      {
        driver = new FirefoxDriver();
      }

      @After
      public void cleanup()
      {
          driver.close();
          driver.quit();
      }
}
```

Below is the sample test class. In below test class, we have created a simple test to verify the title of website - www.softpost.org

```java
package seleniumtests;

import org.junit.Assert;
import org.junit.Test;

public class SmokeTests extends BaseTest
{

    @Test
    public void verifyTitle()
    {
        driver.get("http://www.softpost.org");

Assert.assertTrue(driver.getTitle().contains("F
ree Software Tutorials"));
    }
}
```

After this, all you need to do is push this project on GitHub or your local repository server.
Then on Bamboo, you need to create maven build

22. Selenium in Cloud

22.1 Testing web applications in Cloud with SauceLabs

Here is the sample code to invoke the driver on SauceLabs server.

```
String URL = "http://" + UserId+ ":" +
Access_Key +
"@ondemand.saucelabs.com:80/wd/hub";
WebDriver driver = new RemoteWebDriver(new
URL(URL), caps);
```

To test the web applications hosted on local servers, you need to download and execute the Sauce Connect. Sauce Connect is an application that creates a secure tunnel connection between the Sauce Labs Cloud and the host from where you are executing the tests. It also allows you to pass through firewall.

sc.exe -u xyz -k anykey --proxy 1.11.1.11:8080 --proxy-userpwd userid:passwd --pac http://pqr

Here is the sample example -

```
import org.junit.Test;
import org.openqa.selenium.By;
import org.openqa.selenium.WebDriver;
import
org.openqa.selenium.remote.DesiredCapabilities;
import
org.openqa.selenium.remote.RemoteWebDriver;
import java.net.MalformedURLException;
import java.net.URL;
import java.util.Random;
```

```
/**
 * Created by Sagar on 03-07-2016.
 */
public class BrowserStackTests
{
    String Access_Key = "myxyzkey";
    String UserId = "reply2sagar";
    String url="http://"+UserId+":"+Access_Key
+"@ondemand.saucelabs.com:80/wd/hub";

    @Test
    public void testIPhone()
    {
        DesiredCapabilities caps = new
DesiredCapabilities();
        caps.setCapability("appiumVersion",
"1.5.3");
        caps.setCapability("deviceName","iPhone
6");
        caps.setCapability("deviceOrientation",
"portrait");

caps.setCapability("platformVersion","9.3");
        caps.setCapability("platformName",
"iOS");
        caps.setCapability("browserName",
"Safari");
        caps.setCapability("name", "iPhone 6
Test");
        caps.setCapability("build", 11);

        try
        {
            WebDriver driver = new
RemoteWebDriver(new URL(url), caps);

driver.get("http://www.softpost.org/selenium-
test-page/");
```

```
driver.findElement(By.id("fn")).sendKeys("Sagar
");
            driver.close();
            driver.quit();
    }catch (MalformedURLException ex){
            System.out.println("Malformed
Exception");
        }
    }

    @Test
    public void testIpad()
    {
        DesiredCapabilities caps = new
DesiredCapabilities();
        caps.setCapability("appiumVersion",
"1.5.3");
        caps.setCapability("deviceName","iPad
2");
        caps.setCapability("deviceOrientation",
"portrait");

caps.setCapability("platformVersion","9.3");
        caps.setCapability("platformName",
"iOS");
        caps.setCapability("browserName",
"Safari");
        caps.setCapability("name", "iPad 2
Test");
        caps.setCapability("build", 12);

        try
        {
            WebDriver driver = new
RemoteWebDriver(new URL(url), caps);

driver.get("http://www.softpost.org/selenium-
test-page/");
```

```
driver.findElement(By.id("fn")).sendKeys("Sagar
");
            driver.close();
            driver.quit();
        }
    catch (MalformedURLException ex)
    {
            System.out.println("Malformed
Exception");
    }
  }
}
```

After you execute code locally, you will see the tests running on Sacuelabs VMs at below url.
https://saucelabs.com/beta/dashboard/builds

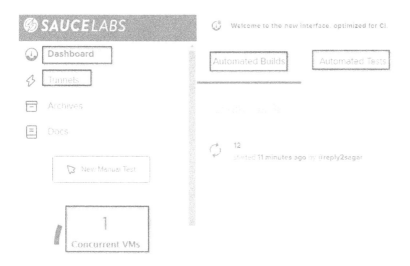

22.2 Running Selenium tests in Cloud with BrowserStack

BrowserStack is the company which provides running of web tests on various platforms and browsers in the cloud. It supports various platforms and OS as mentioned below.

1. OS - windows, linux, OSX, iOS, Android
2. Browsers - chrome, IE, Firefox, Opera, Safari
3. Device - iPhone 5, Samsung galaxy, iPad

We provide the username/access key + driver capabilities to BrowserStack and they provide us with the driver with specified capabilities. In below example - We are requesting the IE driver on Windows OS. BrowserStack provides the sample capabilities code as well.

```
String URL = "https://" + USER_ID + ":" +
ACCESS_KEY +
"@hub-cloud.browserstack.com/wd/hub";
    DesiredCapabilities caps = new
DesiredCapabilities();
    caps.setCapability("os", "Windows");
    caps.setCapability("os_version", "XP");
    caps.setCapability("browser", "IE");
    caps.setCapability("browser_version",
"7.0");

    WebDriver driver = new RemoteWebDriver(new
URL(URL), caps);
```

Testing web applications hosted on local servers

If the web application you are testing is in public domain, you do not need to do any extra set up. But if your application is accessible in only your local network, you need to run the binary so that cloud network of

BrowserStack can access your local servers through secured connection. This binary can be downloaded here(https://www.browserstack.com/automate/java#setting-local-tunnel).

You can execute binary using below syntax.

BrowserStackLocal.exe key -forcelocal -proxyHost 1.1.1.1 - proxyPort 8080 -proxyUser user -proxyPass password - localIdentifier localWindows

After running the binary, ensure that you also pass below capability.

```
caps.setCapability("browserstack.local",
"true");
```

BrowserStack Specific Capabilities

Here is the list of some BrowserStack Specific Capabilities

1. caps.setCapability("build", "B1");
2. caps.setCapability("project", "Softpost");
3. caps.setCapability("browserstack.ie.noFlash", "true");
4. caps.setCapability("browserstack.ie.enablePopups", "true");
5. caps.setCapability("browserstack.safari.enablePopups", "true");
6. caps.setCapability("browserstack.debug", "true");

Taking screenshot on BrowserStack

```
driver = (RemoteWebDriver) new
Augmenter().augment(driver);
File file1= (File) ((TakesScreenshot)
driver).getScreenshotAs(OutputType.FILE);
FileUtils.copyFile(file1, new File("abc.png"));
```

Automating website that asks for authentication

```
driver.get("https://user:password@www.softpost.
org");
```

Setting proxy server settings

```
System.getProperties().put("http.proxyHost",
"proxyhost");
System.getProperties().put("http.proxyPort",
"8080");
System.getProperties().put("http.proxyUser",
"proxyuser");
System.getProperties().put("http.proxyPassword"
, "proxy-password");

//For HTTPS servers, we can use below syntax.
System.getProperties().put("https.proxyHost",
"proxyhost");
System.getProperties().put("https.proxyPort",
"8080");
System.getProperties().put("https.proxyUser",
"proxyuser");
System.getProperties().put("https.proxyPassword
", "proxy-password");
```

Here is the complete example on BrowserStack.

```java
import org.junit.Test;
import org.openqa.selenium.By;
import org.openqa.selenium.WebDriver;
import org.openqa.selenium.remote.DesiredCapabilities;
import org.openqa.selenium.remote.RemoteWebDriver;
import java.net.MalformedURLException;
import java.net.URL;
import java.util.Random;

/**
 * Created by Sagar on 03-07-2016.
 */
public class BrowserStackTests
{
    String Access_Key = "mykey";
    String UserId = "sagar211";
    String url = "http://" + UserId+ ":" +
Access_Key +"@hub-
cloud.browserstack.com/wd/hub";

    @Test
    public void testIPhone()
    {
        DesiredCapabilities caps = new
DesiredCapabilities();
        caps.setCapability("browserName",
"iPhone");
        caps.setCapability("platform", "MAC");
        caps.setCapability("device", "iPhone
6S");

        try
        {
            WebDriver driver = new
RemoteWebDriver(new URL(url), caps);
```

```
driver.get("http://www.softpost.org/selenium-
test-page/");

driver.findElement(By.id("fn")).sendKeys("Sagar
");
            driver.close();
            driver.quit();
        }
        catch (MalformedURLException ex)
        {
            System.out.println("Malformed
Exception");
        }
    }

    @Test
    public void testIpad()
    {
        DesiredCapabilities caps = new
DesiredCapabilities();
        caps.setCapability("browserName",
"iPad");
        caps.setCapability("platform", "MAC");
        caps.setCapability("device", "iPad
Pro");

        try
        {
            WebDriver driver = new
RemoteWebDriver(new URL(url), caps);

driver.get("http://www.softpost.org/selenium-
test-page/");

driver.findElement(By.id("fn")).sendKeys("Sagar
");
            driver.close();
            driver.quit();
        }
```

```
        catch (MalformedURLException ex)
        {
                System.out.println("Malformed
Exception");
        }
    }
    @Test
    public void testAndroid()
    {
        DesiredCapabilities caps = new
DesiredCapabilities();
        caps.setCapability("browserName",
"android");
        caps.setCapability("platform",
"ANDROID");
        caps.setCapability("device", "Samsung
Galaxy S5");

        try
         {
            WebDriver driver = new
RemoteWebDriver(new URL(url), caps);

driver.get("http://www.softpost.org/selenium-
test-page/");

driver.findElement(By.id("fn")).sendKeys("Sagar
");
            driver.quit();
        }catch (MalformedURLException ex){
            System.out.println("Malformed
Exception");
        }
    }
}
```

You can watch your tests executing on below url.
https://www.browserstack.com/automate

Below image shows how the BrowserStack dashboard looks like.

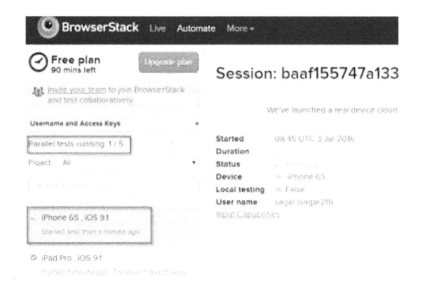

23. Mobile application testing

23.1 First Mobile Automation test using Appium

What is Appium?

Appium is a mobile automation testing tool used to test android and IOS applications.

Installation and Setting up of Environment for running Appium tests

Please follow below steps to set up the environment.

1. Download and Install Java. Set up JAVA_HOME and JRE_HOME.
2. Download and Install Android SDK. Set up ANDROID_HOME.
3. Also configure system path variable to include Java and Android tools.
4. Download and Extract Appium.
5. Set up device (Virtual device or Android phone) on which tests have to be run. If you are using real Android phone for testing then please enable developer option by tapping on the version menu (found in settings->About device) 7 times. Once Developer option is made visible, you should enable usb debugging. Then you can attach your device to laptop using usb cable. For the first time, your device mac address will be registered in device manager, You also need to accept a message to acknowledge the registration on your phone.

First Program to test Calculator using Appium

You can run write your tests in any language like Java, C#.Net, PHP, Python etc. Below program uses C#.Net language.

```
using System;
using
Microsoft.VisualStudio.TestTools.UnitTesting;
using System;
using
Microsoft.VisualStudio.TestTools.UnitTesting;
using OpenQA.Selenium.Chrome;
using OpenQA.Selenium.Remote;
using OpenQA.Selenium.Support;
using OpenQA.Selenium;
using System.Text.RegularExpressions;

namespace Appium
{
    [TestClass]
    public class UnitTest2
    {
        [TestMethod]
        public void TestMethod1()
        {

        IWebDriver driver;
 DesiredCapabilities capabilities = new
DesiredCapabilities();
 capabilities.SetCapability("BROWSER_Name",
"Android");
 capabilities.SetCapability("VERSION",
"4.4.4");

capabilities.SetCapability("deviceName","yource
llname");
```

```
capabilities.SetCapability("platformName","Andr
oid");

    capabilities.SetCapability("appPackage",
"com.sec.android.app.popupcalculator");

capabilities.SetCapability("appActivity","com.s
ec.android.app.popupcalculator.Calculator");
    driver = new RemoteWebDriver(new
Uri("http://127.0.0.1:4723/wd/hub"),
capabilities);

    //locate the Text on the calculator by using
By.Name()
    driver.FindElement(By.Name("3")).Click();

    driver.FindElement(By.Name("+")).Click();

    driver.FindElement(By.Name("5")).Click();

    driver.FindElement(By.Name("=")).Click();
    IWebElement txt=
driver.FindElement(By.ClassName("android.widget
.EditText"));

    String p = txt.Text.ToString();
    String replacement = Regex.Replace(p,
@"\t|\n|\r", "");
    Assert.AreEqual(replacement, "3+5=8",
txt.Text);
 driver.Quit();


        }
     }
}
```

Running First Program to test Calculator using Appium

Please follow below steps to run above test using Appium.

1. Launch Appium Application by double clicking on Appium exe file.
2. Start the server.
3. Attach your device in debug mode.
4. Run the program and see the magic!! Calculator application is launched on your device and sum of 3 and 5 is done.

Difference between Appium and Selendroid

Appium can be used to test android as well as iOS based application. Selendroid can be used to test only Android based applications. Selendroid can test application developed using API level 17 and below. But Appium can only test application developed using API level 17 and above. We can record steps using inspector tool in Selendroid. We can use UI automater viewer tool in Android SDK to inspect the elements of application.

23.2 Mobile emulation using chrome

Below example illustrates how to execute the Selenium tests on iPhone 5 S using mobile emulation feature provided in chrome. Similarly we can run tests on other devices like Apple iPad, Google Nexus 5 etc.

```java
package browsertests;

import org.junit.Test;
import org.openqa.selenium.WebDriver;
import org.openqa.selenium.chrome.ChromeDriver;
import
org.openqa.selenium.chrome.ChromeOptions;
import
org.openqa.selenium.remote.DesiredCapabilities;

import java.util.HashMap;
import java.util.Map;

/**
 * Created by sagar on 06-12-2015.
 */
public class MobileEmulationOnChrome
{
    @Test
    public void launchChrome()
    {
        Map<String, String> mobileEmulation =
new HashMap<String, String>();
        // mobileEmulation.put("deviceName",
"Google Nexus 5");
        mobileEmulation.put("deviceName",
"Apple iPhone 5");
        //mobileEmulation.put("deviceName",
"Apple iPad");
        Map<String, Object> chromeOptions = new
HashMap<String, Object>();
        chromeOptions.put("mobileEmulation",
mobileEmulation);
```

```
        DesiredCapabilities capabilities =
DesiredCapabilities.chrome();

capabilities.setCapability(ChromeOptions.CAPABI
LITY, chromeOptions);

System.setProperty("webdriver.chrome.driver","G
:\\softwares\\selenium\\chromedriver2.2.exe");

        WebDriver driver = new
ChromeDriver(capabilities);
        driver.get("http://softpost.org");
        driver.quit();
    }
}
```

23.3 Selendroid - Android application testing tool

What is Selendroid?

Selendroid is an android application testing tool.

Setting up environment

1. Download and Install Java. Set up JAVA_HOME and JRE_HOME. Download and Install Android SDK. For example - D:\Program Files\Java\jdk1.8.0_45
2. Set up ANDROID_HOME. Also configure system path variable to include Java and Android tools. For example D:\Android\sdk
3. Set up device (Virtual device or Android phone) on which tests have to be run. If you are using real Android phone for testing then please enable developer option by tapping on the version menu

(found in settings->About device) 7 times. Once Developer option becomes visible, you should enable usb debugging. Then you can attach your device to laptop using usb cable. For the first time, your device mac address will be registered in device manager, You also need to accept a message with RSA key fingerprint to acknowledge the registration on your phone. To check that your device is up and running, you must run the command - "adb devices". This command displays all the devices attached to computer.

4. Download Selendroid jar files and test apk application.

First program to test application using Selendroid

```java
import io.selendroid.client.SelendroidDriver;
import io.selendroid.common.SelendroidCapabilities;
import org.openqa.selenium.WebDriver;

public class Sele
{
 /**
  * @param args
  */
 public static void main(String[] args) throws
Exception
 {
  WebDriver driver;
  SelendroidCapabilities x;
  x = new
SelendroidCapabilities("io.selendroid.testapp:0
.15.0");
  driver = new SelendroidDriver(x);
 }
}
```

Running First program using Selendroid

1. Run the command java -jar selendroid.jar -aut selendroid-test.apk. You should see the server running at http://localhost:4444/wd/hub/status
2. then run above code.

Troubleshooting Issues

1. To fix the error - "Error occurred while resigning the app selendroid - set the Java_home to home directory.
2. You may see error saying "The requested application under test is not configured in selendroid server. - select correct app id from url". To fix this error, make sure that you have given correct app id.
3. emulator: ERROR: x86 emulation currently requires hardware acceleration! This error comes when you try to launch virtual device. To fix this you will need to install Intel HAXM software.

Other important points to consider –

1. You need to download Selendroid client jar file from http://repo1.maven.org/maven2/io/selendroid/selendroid-client/0.15.0/ - download client. This is required as SelendroidDriver class and other classes are defined inside it.
2. You can use tool at below url to inspect the application structure. http://localhost:4444/inspector

Important Android tools –

1. **Android device monitor** shows all devices attached to computer and also gives details about app package name, activity name and also we can view the app structure and code
2. **With AVD Manager**, we can manage android devices, attach new devices.
3. **With SDK Manager**, we can install/uninstall android api packages.
4. with chrome://inspect/#devices, you can inspect web apps in chrome –

Below screenshot shows the device monitor.

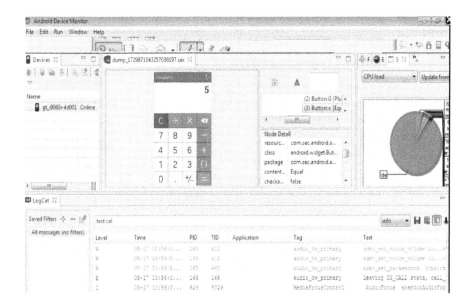

24. Selenium grid

24.1 RemoteWebdriver in Selenium

You will need to use RemoteWebdriver if you want to connect to selenium server. We pass the capabilities to remote server which passes the commands to appropriate machine where the driver with given capabilities is available.

RemoteWebdriver is mainly useful when you are using Selenium Grid or running tests in Cloud.
One of the constructors of RemoteWebdriver takes 2 parameters - url of selenium server and capabilities

24.2 Selenium Grid

Selenium grid allows you to run the same tests on different platforms in parallel. Just imagine that you have a web application that can be accessed from desktop, laptop, iPad, iPhone, Android phone or any other mobile device.

Testing the same application on all these platforms is a challenging task and time consuming as well. But with Selenium Grid you can test your application on various platforms very quickly. The beauty about selenium is that you do not need to write different code for running tests on various configurations. Same selenium code works on all platforms.

Components of Selenium Grid -

1. Hub - Selenium Server - Passes on JSON commands to capable nodes. A single HUB controls all nodes. HUB knows what are the capabilities of each node are like OS, browser etc.
2. Node - Selenium Server driving actual browser. On node actual automation execution happens. Each node registers itself with the HUB.
3. Test machine - Where your test code is executed.

Steps in Selenium Grid automation execution

1. You run your selenium code from editor like IntelliJ IDEA or eclipse
2. Your code send http commands to HUB including information like what the desired capabilities are. For example - you may ask for remote webdriver that can run tests on Windows OS and chrome browser.
3. HUB reads the capabilities information and forwards the commands to the capable node.
4. Node creates a new session and returns the result to HUB.
5. HUB returns the result to your code.
6. All other commands are executed in the same session

Starting Hub

You can start the hub using below command.

```
java -jar server.jar -role hub
```

You can also use the below command to start the hub with json configuration

```
java -jar server.jar -role hub -hubConfig
myconfig.json
```

Starting Node

You can start the node using below command.

```
java -jar server.jar -role node -hub
http://localhost:4444/grid/register -port 3333
```

You can also register the node using json file.

```
java -jar server.jar -role node -nodeConfig
myconfig.json
```

Here is the sample node configuration json file.

```
{
"capabilities":
            [
                {
```

```
                                "platform":
"WINDOWS",

                                "browserName":
"chrome",

                                "maxInstances":
1,

                                "seleniumProtoc
ol": "WebDriver"
                },
                {
                                "platform":
"WINDOWS",

                                "browserName":
"firefox",

                                "maxInstances":
1,

                                "seleniumProtoc
ol": "WebDriver"
                },
                {
                                "platform":
"WINDOWS",

                                "browserName":
"internet explorer",

                                "maxInstances":
1,

                                "seleniumProtoc
ol": "WebDriver"
```

```
                }
                ],
    "configuration":
                {
                                        "cleanUpCycle":
6000,
                                        "registerCycle"
: 6000,
                                        "nodeTimeout":
1000,
                                        "timeout":
500000,
                                        "nodePolling":
3000,
                                        "hub":
"http://localhost:4444/grid/register",
                                        "proxy":
"org.openqa.grid.selenium.proxy.DefaultRemotePr
oxy",
                                        "maxSession": 2,
                                        "port": 6666,
                                        "host":
"nodeName",
                                        "register":
true,
                                        "hubPort": 4444,
                                        "hubHost"
:"localhost",
```

```
            "role": "node"

        }
}
```

```
PS C:\Users\Sagar\Downloads> java -jar server.jar -role node -hub http://
localhost:4444/grid/register -port 3333
17:47:38.522 INFO - Launching a Selenium Grid node
17:47:40.946 INFO - Java: Oracle Corporation 25.91-b14
17:47:40.947 INFO - OS: Windows 10 10.0 amd64
17:47:40.962 INFO - v2.53.1, with Core v2.53.1. Built from revision a36b8
b1
17:47:41.127 INFO - Driver class not found: com.opera.core.systems.OperaD
river
17:47:41.128 INFO - Driver provider com.opera.core.systems.OperaDriver is
 not registered
17:47:41.142 INFO - Driver provider org.openqa.selenium.safari.SafariDriv
er registration is skipped:
registration capabilities Capabilities [{browserName=safari, version=, pl
atform=MAC}] does not match the current platform WIN10
17:47:41.145 INFO - Driver class not found: org.openqa.selenium.htmlunit.
HtmlUnitDriver
17:47:41.146 INFO - Driver provider org.openqa.selenium.htmlunit.HtmlUnit
Driver is not registered
17:47:41.231 INFO - Version Jetty/5.1.x
17:47:41.234 INFO - Started HttpContext[/selenium-server,/selenium-server
]
17:47:41.237 INFO - Started org.openqa.jetty.jetty.servlet.ServletHandler
@120d6fe6
17:47:41.238 INFO - Started HttpContext[/wd,/wd]
17:47:41.239 INFO - Started HttpContext[/selenium-server/driver,/selenium
-server/driver]
17:47:41.239 INFO - Started SocketListener on 0.0.0.0:3333
17:47:41.244 INFO - Started org.openqa.jetty.jetty.Server@1f57539
17:47:41.246 INFO - Selenium Grid node is up and ready to register to the
 hub
17:47:41.310 INFO - Starting auto registration thread. Will try to regist
er every 5000 ms.
17:47:41.311 INFO - Registering the node to the hub: http://localhost:444
4/grid/register
17:47:41.395 INFO - The node is registered to the hub and ready to use
```

Once Hub and node is up and running, you can view your grid at below url
http://localhost:4444/grid/console

254

To register the Appium node you can use below command.

```
appium --nodeconfig mynodeconfig.json
```

Here is the sample iPhone node config file.

```
{
    "capabilities": [
        {
            "browserName": "iPhone-Simulator",
            "version": "7.1",
            "maxInstances": 1,
            "platform": "MAC"
        }
    ],
    "configuration": {
        "cleanUpCycle": 3000,
        "timeout": 400000,
      "browserTimeout": 70000,
        "hub":
"http://localhost:4444/grid/register",
        "host": " iPhoneHostName",
        "maxSession": 1,
        "port": 1234,
        "hubPort": 4444,
        "hubHost": " localhost",
        "url":
"http:// iPhoneHostName:1234/wd/hub",
        "register": true,
```

```
        "registerCycle": 6000,
         "role": "node"
    }
}
```

Here is the sample json configuration file for Android

```
{
"capabilities":
[
{
"deviceName": "sagarcell",
"browserName": "Android",
"version":"4.4.4",
"maxInstances": 1,
"platform":"ANDROID"
}
],
"configuration":
{
"cleanUpCycle":300000,
"timeout":400000,
"proxy":
"org.openqa.grid.selenium.proxy.DefaultRemotePr
oxy",
"url":"http://appium:4730/wd/hub",
"maxSession": 1,
```

```
"port": "4730",
"host": "appium",
"register": true,
"registerCycle": 3000,
"hubPort": "4444",
"hubHost": "127.0.0.1"
}
}
```

Executing Code

Below example shows how to execute the selenium tests in Grid.

```java
package browsertests;
import org.junit.Test;
import org.openqa.selenium.WebDriver;
import
org.openqa.selenium.remote.DesiredCapabilities;
import
org.openqa.selenium.remote.RemoteWebDriver;
import java.net.URL;
import java.util.concurrent.TimeUnit;
public class TestFirefoxGrid
{
    private WebDriver driver;
```

```
    @Test
    public void loadingSinglePageTest() throws
Exception
    {
       driver = new RemoteWebDriver(new
URL("http://localhost:4444/wd/hub"),
       DesiredCapabilities.firefox());
 driver.manage().timeouts().implicitlyWait(20,
TimeUnit.SECONDS);
    driver.get("http://www.softpost.org");
    driver.quit();
        //quit the browser
    }
}
```

Below example shows how to execute the selenium tests
on Android phone in Grid.

```
package browsertests;
import org.junit.Test;
import org.openqa.selenium.WebDriver;
import
org.openqa.selenium.remote.DesiredCapabilities;
import
org.openqa.selenium.remote.RemoteWebDriver;
import java.net.URL;
import java.util.concurrent.TimeUnit;
```

```java
public class LaunchWebsiteOnAndroidPhoneGrid
{
    private WebDriver driver;
    @Test
    public void loadingSinglePageTest() throws
Exception
    {
        DesiredCapabilities capabilities = new
DesiredCapabilities();
capabilities.setCapability("platformName",
"ANDROID");
capabilities.setCapability("platformVersion",
"4.4.4");
capabilities.setCapability("browserName",
"MobileBrowserType.BROWSER");
capabilities.setCapability("app", "chrome");
  WebDriver driver = new RemoteWebDriver(new
URL("http://localhost:4444/wd/hub"),capabilitie
s);
driver.manage().timeouts().implicitlyWait(20,
TimeUnit.SECONDS);
  driver.get("http://www.softpost.org");
  driver.quit();
   //quit the browser
    }
}
```

25. Comparing selenium with other tools

25.1 Difference between Selenium Webdriver and UFT (QTP)

Selenium and QTP , both of them are automation testing tools.

Major difference between QTP and Selenium are :

1. Selenium is an open source tool while QTP is not an open source tool. It is owned by the HP.
2. Selenium is used to test only web based applications while QTP can be used to test wide variety of applications like web based, .net based, Java based, mainframe applications.
3. Selenium supports scripting in many different languages like Java, .Net, Python, Ruby etc While in QTP only vb scripting is provided.
4. Web automation testing with selenium requires less cost as compared to automation using QTP due to license cost.

25.2 Difference between Selenium and Lean FT

Here is the main difference between Selenium and LeanFT

1. Selenium is open source. LeanFT is licensed tool developed by HP
2. Selenium can be used to automate only Web applications. LeanFT can be used to automate web as well as desktop applications
3. Selenium uses the locators like XPATH, CSS. LeanFT uses properties and value pairs. But we can also use XPATH
4. Selenium is better in cross browser testing than LeanFT
5. Both are platform independent.
6. LeanFT scripts can be developed in only Java and C#. Selenium scripts can be written many languages like Java, C#, Perl, PHP, Python, Ruby, JavaScript etc.

25.3 Difference between Selenium and Appium

Here is the comparison between Selenium and Appium

1. Selenium is an open source tool to test web applications running in desktop browsers. Appium is an open source tool to test the web applications running in mobile browsers. Appium also supports automation of native and hybrid mobile applications developed for iOS and Android OS. Appium uses selenium API to test the applications.
2. Appium wraps vendor specific API into Webdriver API which is common for automating all types of mobile browsers. For example - Android API is different than iOS API. But Webdriver API is same. That's what Appium does for you!

3. Appium can be used to test applications on various devices and platforms like Android phones, Apple iPads, Apple iPhones etc

Below image shows the difference between Selenium and Appium.

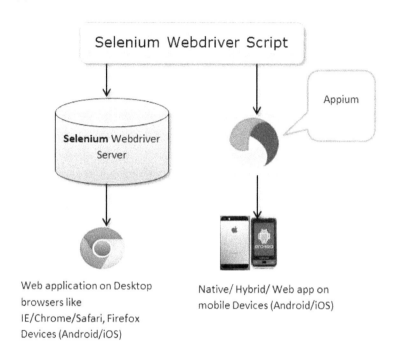

Web application on Desktop browsers like IE/Chrome/Safari, Firefox Devices (Android/iOS)

Native/ Hybrid/ Web app on mobile Devices (Android/iOS)

26.Challenges in Selenium automation

26.1 Limitations of Selenium

Even though Selenium is the most popular automation testing tool, it has got below limitations.

1. We can only test web applications. We can not test desktop based applications.
2. We can test mobile applications but we need to use the Appium for that.
3. We can not automate the CAPTCHA
4. We can not automate the complex control like Flash, Silver light Components, Applet controls, native window dialogs etc
5. We often encounter issues like Selenium not launching latest browsers due to incompatibility issues. In such scenarios, we have to downgrade the browser in order to automate it.

26.2 Handling windows dialog using AutoIT

Some times you will have to handle the file upload window using selenium web driver.
Selenium does not provide any such way to handle the window pop ups.

You can use AutoIT script to automate this task. AutoIT is a scripting language for Microsoft windows applications. You will have to download and install AutoIT from this url Download AutoIT

Once downloaded, you can write below code in the script

file and invoke that file code just when you need to handle the upload window. Semicolon(;) is used to mark the comments in AutoIT scripts.

```
;below line states Windows controller to wait
for the window with title Open to display.
Whatever is the name of window, you need to
pass it here.

WinWaitActive("Open")

;below line will enter the file location to be
uploaded.
Send("C:\Users\sagar\Documents\onion_fennel_bis
que.jpg")

;finally we need to click on Ok or press enter
to start the upload process.
Send("{ENTER}")
```

Here is the complete example.

```
package seleniumtest;

//autoIT
//TestNG
//Grid

//import the required classes
import java.text.SimpleDateFormat;
import java.util.Date;
import java.util.Set;
import java.util.concurrent.TimeUnit;
import org.openqa.selenium.By;
import org.openqa.selenium.WebDriver;
import org.openqa.selenium.*;
import org.openqa.selenium.chrome.ChromeDriver;

public   class AutoIT
{
  public static void main(String[] args)
  {
      WebDriver driver =null;
     //set the driver path
  System.setProperty("webdriver.chrome.driver",
 "F:\\selenium\\csharp\\chromedriver.exe");
  System.setProperty("webdriver.ie.driver",
"F:\\selenium\\IEDriverServer_Win32_2.43.0\\IED
riverServer.exe");
```

```
  Date dNow = new Date( );
  //create new driver instance
    driver = new ChromeDriver();
 driver.manage().timeouts().pageLoadTimeout(60,
TimeUnit.SECONDS);
  driver.manage().timeouts().implicitlyWait(20,
TimeUnit.SECONDS);
      try
      {
driver.get("https://www.pdftoword.com/");
driver.findElement(By.id("file-
uploader")).click();
 //please note that below line calls the AutoIT
 script which will handle the file upload
dialog in google chrome browser.Also note that
we need to provide the path of exe file which
is created after we compile and build the
AutoIT script.

Runtime.getRuntime().exec("F:\\selenium\\handle
file1.exe");
    //wait for 2 seconds
    Thread.sleep(5000);
    }
  catch(Exception e)
    {
     //print exception if any
    System.out.println(e.getMessage() );
```

```
    e.printStackTrace();
 }
  finally
   {
    //close the driver
  driver.close();
  //quit the driver.
  driver.quit();
  }
 }
}
```

www.ingramcontent.com/pod-product-compliance
Lightning Source LLC
Chambersburg PA
CBHW071545080326
40689CB00061B/1858